Modeling Reserve Recruiting

Estimates of Enlistments

Jeremy Arkes, M. Rebecca Kilburn

Prepared for the Office of the Secretary of Defense

NATIONAL DEFENSE RESEARCH INSTITUTE

The research described in this report was prepared for the Office of the Secretary of Defense (OSD). The research was conducted in the RAND National Defense Research Institute, a federally funded research and development center supported by the OSD, the Joint Staff, the unified commands, and the defense agencies under Contract DASW01-01-C-0004.

Library of Congress Cataloging-in-Publication Data

Arkes, Jeremy.
    Modeling reserve recruiting : estimates of enlistments / Jeremy Arkes, M. Rebecca Kilburn.
      p. cm.
    Includes bibliographical references.
    "MG-202."
    ISBN 0-8330-3820-6 (pbk. : alk. paper)
    1. United States—Armed Forces—Reserves—Estimates. 2. Manpower planning—United States—
Mathematical models. 3. United States—Armed Forces—Recruiting, enlistment, etc. I. Kilburn, M. Rebecca.
II.Title.

UA42.A7156 2005
355.3'7'0973—dc22

2005017311

Published 2005 by the RAND Corporation
1776 Main Street, P.O. Box 2138, Santa Monica, CA 90407-2138
1200 South Hayes Street, Arlington, VA 22202-5050
201 North Craig Street, Suite 202, Pittsburgh, PA 15213-1516
RAND URL: http://www.rand.org/
To order RAND documents or to obtain additional information, contact
Distribution Services: Telephone: (310) 451-7002;
Fax: (310) 451-6915; Email: order@rand.org

Preface

Reserve components are increasingly being called upon to provide support across the entire spectrum of military operations and have been key to operations in Iraq and Afghanistan. Therefore, the issue of their readiness is critical for national military strategy. The Office of the Secretary of Defense (Accession Policy Directorate) felt that the time was appropriate for an examination of reserve recruiting and the likely challenges facing the reserve components in the future.

The RAND Corporation was asked to undertake a study of reserve recruiting with the ultimate aim of improving the Defense Department's ability to forecast supply and foreshadow potential problems. The first report from the study (currently unpublished RAND research by M. Rebecca Kilburn, Sheila Nataraj Kirby, C. Christine Fair, and Scott Naftel) describes trends in the recruiting environment that would be expected to affect reserve recruiting and the theoretical model. The present monograph reports on the results of the second portion of the project and focuses on estimating models for reserve recruiting. Although the analysis was performed prior to the recent military engagements in Afghanistan and Iraq, the results should be of interest to those concerned about military recruiting and reserve force issues, given the current military environment, as well as to the larger defense manpower research community.

This report was prepared under the sponsorship of the Office of Accession Policy, Office of the Under Secretary of Defense for Personnel and Readiness. It was prepared within the Forces and Resources Policy Center of the RAND National Defense Research Institute, a federally funded research and development center sponsored by the Office of the Secretary of Defense, the Joint Staff, the Unified Combatant Commands, the Department of the Navy, the Marine Corps, the defense agencies, and the defense Intelligence Community.

For more information on RAND's Forces and Resources Policy Center, contact the Acting Director, James Hosek. He can be reached by email at James_Hosek@rand.org; by phone at 310-393-0411, extension 7183; or by mail at the RAND Corporation, 1776 Main Street, Santa Monica, California 90407-2138. More information about RAND is available at www.rand.org.

Contents

Figures

Tables

Summary

As reserve forces have become more important to military operations, reserve recruiting has faced many of the same challenges that have confronted recruiting for the active forces. These include more attractive civilian opportunities and a declining propensity among youth to join the ranks of military service. An additional challenge for the reserves is the shrinking active duty force, from which the reserves draw two-thirds of their members.

Despite the growing importance of the reserves, research on reserve recruiting has received much less attention than active duty recruiting. For about two decades, researchers estimated models of active duty recruiting, variously referred to as "enlistment supply models" or "aggregate recruiting models." These models typically examine how labor market factors, demographic factors, and recruiting policies influence enlistment in the active duty.

Given the growing importance of reserve recruiting, the Office of the Secretary of Defense asked RAND to assess the feasibility of this type of estimating model for reserve recruiting. In the first portion of this effort, we reviewed trends in reserve recruiting and the civilian factors that influence recruiting, and we recommended updates to the active duty models of enlistment supply based on the reserve recruiting process and these trends. These results are currently unpublished RAND research by M. Rebecca Kilburn, Sheila Nataraj Kirby, C. Christine Fair, and Scott Naftel. In this monograph, we describe available data and the strategies we used to create models to estimate reserve recruiting, report the results from the models, and discuss the policy implications of the estimates.

Our work incorporates four features that we believe provide a more realistic representation of reserve recruiting than previous research has done. Specifically, we

- account for the possibility that individuals without prior service may choose active service, reserve duty, or civilian opportunities, rather than the typical approach of choosing to enlist in active duty or the reserves separately
- consider education as well as work among the alternatives to enlistment
- recognize that men are devoting increased amounts of time to family life, which may restrict the amount of time they would be willing to give to the reserves
- incorporate the effects that role models may have on recruiting.

After three straight years of failing to meet its goal for recruiting reserves, the Department of Defense (DoD) met its goal for FY 2000, thanks largely to accessions among individuals with no prior military service. About two-thirds of reserve accessions are by individuals with prior active duty service. Such accessions were below the FY 2000 goal, but this shortfall was offset by accessions among non-prior-service (NPS) individuals that exceeded

DoD goals. Active duty components also recruit NPS individuals and may compete with the reserve components for these recruits.

Developing a Model and Objective

Recruiting models can be used to predict the number of recruits the military is likely to receive in future years or to identify what labor market, demographic, and policy variables are most likely to affect recruiting. Because our goal is to identify the relationships between these variables and recruiting outcomes, we developed a model that would yield optimal properties of coefficient estimates for the effects of different variables.

We developed two separate models, one each for individuals with and without prior service. Our data set included observations from 50 states and the District of Columbia for the years 1992 through 1999, resulting in 408 "state-FY" cases for observation. At the time of the analysis, many of the variables we selected were not available before 1992, and updated information on some was not available after 1999.

Model Variables and Their Predicted Effects

For each of these 408 observations, we compiled statistics on variables most likely to affect a decision to enlist. For example, we hypothesize that higher civilian wages would encourage a potential recruit to seek civilian employment over active duty enlistment, while higher civilian unemployment rates could influence a youth to select military service. More general hypothesized relationships, and some of the variables we selected to test them, include the following.

Economic Variables

We expect that a stronger economy would reduce the number of recruits for active duty because of better civilian job opportunities. For reserve accessions, economic effects are not clear. A stronger economy would produce more opportunities for second jobs, reducing the number of persons inclined to enter the reserves. At the same time, such an economy could influence persons who would otherwise select active duty to take a civilian job and enlist in the reserves instead. We include unemployment rates and wage levels to measure economic effects.

Demographic Factors

Because enlistment rates of different racial and ethnic groups vary, we expect enlistment rates in areas to vary based on the race and ethnicity of their populations. Hence we include in our model, by state, the percentages of youth who are black or Hispanic.

"Influencer" Variables

In planning for their years after high school, youths typically seek the guidance of their parents and of other "influencers," such as teachers, coaches, and other adult friends. In recent years, as the veteran population has declined, it is likely that the number of influencers with positive, personal military experience who would recommend it to young adults has declined.

To account for this change, we include in our model percentages by state of adults 25 to 65 years of age who are veterans. While the veteran population has declined, the college-educated population, and the number of influencers who may recommend college over military service, has increased. Hence, we also include in our model percentages by state of the population 25–65 with a bachelor's or higher degree.

Civilian Workforce Characteristics

Beyond the opportunity for jobs, the types of jobs that workers hold may influence reserve enlistment. Employer support of participation in the reserves varies by size and type of employer, with larger firms and public employers generally having more flexible policies than other employers for reservists. At the same time, larger firms typically pay higher wages, so people in states with a higher concentration of larger firms may have better alternative opportunities to enlisting. Also, a large public employment base, perceived to be less susceptible to economic fluctuations, could encourage youths to seek public civilian employment rather than military enlistment. To evaluate these factors, we include variables on workers by size of firm and by sector of employment.

Educational Effects

To measure the challenge that colleges can pose to reserve recruiting, we include in our model variables on wages of college graduates and on public college tuition. We also include variables on availability of state merit-based scholarships, such as the Helping Outstanding Pupils Educationally (HOPE) program in Georgia. We expect such programs reduce the number of accessions into both active and reserve forces.

Policy Variables

The DoD may seek to increase recruiting by increasing its advertising, number of recruiters, or bonus programs for recruits. We expect that states with more generous recruiting resources produce more recruits. Given that our model is estimated by state and year, we can include only variables on recruiting resources that vary across state and by year. Because of a lack of data, however, we include just two such variables in our model: the number of active duty recruiters and the availability of state educational incentive programs for members of the National Guard. We were not able to obtain state-level numbers of reserve recruiters.

Research Results

The results we obtained for the model of reserve enlistments by individuals with prior service (PS) largely yielded unreliable results. We believe this unreliability is the result of conceptual and practical problems inherent in assigning a home state to separating PS members. New approaches for PS reserve recruiting estimation models need to be developed that do not rely so heavily on identifying a state for prior active duty members.

Non-Prior-Service Model

The policy variables we included in the NPS model had sizeable and significant effects on both active duty and reserve recruiting. States with educational incentives for National Guard members have higher numbers of both reserve and active duty recruits. In general, at lower levels of recruiter density, both active duty and reserve recruiting benefit from the addition of another recruiter, but as the number of recruiters rise, this benefit becomes successively smaller, eventually becoming negative for reserve recruiting in the range where we observe the bulk of recruiter density. These findings imply that empirical models that just examine the effect of active duty recruiters on active duty recruiting could overstate the net benefits of increasing the number of active duty recruiters from a total force perspective, because reserve recruiting could decrease. Thus, when comparing the cost-effectiveness of various active duty recruiting resources, the impact on reserve recruiting should be considered as well.

Among economic and demographic variables in the NPS model, we found two with a particularly strong relation to recruiting. Higher unemployment rates, not surprisingly, boosted both reserve and active duty recruiting. Minority population prevalence is also a strong predictor of recruiting effort success, including in Hispanic areas.

Our variables on college education had significant but somewhat differing results. First, we found reserve and active duty recruiting lagged in states with scholarship programs similar to the Georgia HOPE program. Such programs initiated over the past decade have been enormously popular; our findings on their effects add to a growing literature on the competition posed by colleges to military recruiting.

Tuition rates had differing effects on active duty and reserve recruiting. States with higher tuition levels had higher percentages of youths enlisting in active duty but lower percentages enlisting in the reserves. This suggests that college is a substitute for active duty but could be a complement to reserve service. There may be opportunities to develop more explicit strategies to attract reservists who would like to couple college studies and military service.

Several economic and demographic variables are noteworthy for their lack of a relationship with recruiting. We did not find varying characteristics of civilian employers to affect recruiting greatly, nor did we find a notable relationship between enlistment and our "influencer" variables. We also found little association between enlistment in the reserves and our measure for the potential demand on men's time for home and family responsibilities.

Acknowledgments

We thank the numerous individuals who helped us during the course of this research. We acknowledge the assistance of the Defense Manpower Data Center—specifically Deborah West, Mike Dove, and Joyce Hamza—for providing us with data used in this report and answering questions related to recruiting data. At RAND, we thank Kanika Kapur for input regarding prediction models and Chris Fair, Charles Lindenblatt, and Jen Sharp for helping obtain additional data used in the analysis. We also thank RAND programmers Jan Hanley and Mark Totten for help processing the data. Thanks are also due Clifford Grammich for writing the summary and research brief for the report. Our reviewers, James Dertouzos and Ron Zimmer, provided useful comments that enhanced the quality of the analysis. We appreciate the help of Carolyn Rogers, Patrice Lester, and Christopher Dirks, who assisted with document preparation.

We very much appreciate the assistance of the following individuals who met with us or provided information about various policies related to reserve recruiting and topics covered in this report: LTC Frank Bryceland, CAPT Mike Ferguson, MAJ Tom Liuzzo, Lt Col Dirk Palmer, Dan Kohner, MAJ Laura Hunter, SMSGT Mary Olson, MAJ Michael Law, and MSGT Frank Harris. In addition, we thank John Stinson, Jr., of the Bureau of Labor Statistics for assisting us in procuring the Multiple Job Holdings data. We appreciate Bob Tinney of Defense Manpower Data Center East for sending us data on the number of active duty recruiters.

Finally, we would like to thank Curtis Gilroy, Director of Accession Policy; Steve Sellman, former Director of Accession Policy; and LTC Frank Bryceland, Col David Kopanski, CAPT Gwen Rutherford, and Robert Clark in the Accession Policy Directorate for their support and comments in conducting this study and preparing this report.

Acronyms

ADMF	Active Duty Master File
AFQT	Armed Forces Qualification Test
CPS	Current Population Survey
DMDC	Defense Manpower Data Center
DoD	Department of Defense
FY	Fiscal year
HOPE	Helping Outstanding Pupils Educationally (Georgia scholarship program)
MEPS	Military Entrance Processing Station
NPS	Non-prior-service
PS	Prior service
RCCPDS	Reserve Components Common Personnel Data System

CHAPTER ONE

Introduction

The reserve forces have increasingly contributed to the total force over the last decade and a half. In fiscal year (FY) 1989 and FY 1990, reservists averaged about one man-day contribution per year to total force operations. By the end of the decade, this contribution had increased more than tenfold, to over 14 man-days per year. Given the recent upswing in the importance of the reserves to the total force, reserve recruiting has received attention more on par with active duty recruiting. Reserve recruiting has faced a number of challenges in the last decade. Primary among these challenges have been the strength of the economy, which has made civilian alternatives to the reserves appear more attractive, and the shrinking of the active force, which has meant a smaller prior-service (PS) pool from which to recruit.

Despite the growing importance of the reserves, research on reserve recruiting has received much less attention than active duty recruiting. For about two decades, researchers estimated active duty recruiting using models variously referred to as "enlistment supply models" or "aggregate recruiting models." These models typically examine how labor market factors, demographic factors, and recruiting policies influence enlistment in the active duty.[1] Examples of this type of study include Cotterman, 1986; Murray and McDonald, 1999; and Warner, Simon, and Payne, 2001.

Given the growing importance of reserve recruiting, the Office of the Secretary of Defense asked RAND to assess the feasibility of estimating reserve recruiting using this type of model. In the first portion of this effort, we reviewed trends in reserve recruiting and the civilian factors that influence recruiting, and we recommended updates to the active duty models of enlistment supply based on the reserve recruiting process and these trends (Kilburn et al., unpublished). In this monograph, we describe available data and the strategies we use to estimate models for reserve recruiting, report the results from the models, and discuss the policy implications of the estimates.

At the same time that the reserves have increasingly been forced to rely on non-prior-service (NPS) recruits, active duty recruiting has faced a number of difficulties. In the late 1990s, active duty recruiting missed recruiting goals. While active duty goals were met in more recent years, the quality of these recruits has declined to levels not seen in over a decade.

Against the backdrop of the increasing importance of the reserves to the total force, shrinking PS pools from which the reserves can recruit, and difficulties faced by active force recruiting, we reconsidered previous recruiting models. Rather than limiting our revisions of recruiting models to minor perturbations of those in the existing literature, we expanded our

---

[1] These types of models are reviewed in Warner and Asch (1995), and we discuss them in more detail below.

options to include a broader rethinking of some of the fundamental features of the models. The result is that we estimate separate models for PS and NPS recruiting because the choice sets and decision frameworks are fundamentally different for the two sets of potential entrants. While the PS model is based on the same concept as previous models, we estimate an NPS model that is truly new in this area of research. Besides separating PS and NPS recruiting, we include the following features in our model that we believe are more realistic representations of the recruiting environment than in prior work on reserve recruiting:

- Our model allows NPS individuals to choose between reserve and active duty enlistment rather than just considering active duty or reserve enlistment in isolation.
- The model considers college attendance in addition to working as an important alternative to enlistment.
- The model recognizes that men are devoting increasing amounts of time to family and that this may be an important source of competition for men's time, particularly for reservists.
- We incorporate the effects that role models may have on recruiting, which is important since more adults in the future will have a college degree and fewer will be veterans.

In sum, the models we estimate in this monograph provide insights into active duty recruiting as well as reserve recruiting, better allow for the fact that active duty and the reserves are often competing for the same NPS individuals, and try to better account for the alternatives to enlistment and the factors that may affect recruiting in the future. Although the analysis was performed prior to the recent Afghanistan and Iraq military engagements, the results should have implications for recruiting in the current environment.

In the next chapter, we provide background information on reserve and active duty recruiting. In Chapter Three, we briefly review the theoretical underpinnings of recruiting models and highlight issues that are particularly important to reserve recruiting. Chapter Four outlines the empirical models we estimate and describes the data. Chapter Five presents results from those estimates, and we highlight policy implications in the final section.

CHAPTER TWO

Background on Recruiting

This chapter provides context for the remainder of the monograph. We discuss the success of reserve and active recruiting over the last decade, the demographic makeup of the reserve components, and trends that would be expected to influence reserve and active duty recruiting.

Recent Recruiting Performance

After three straight years of not meeting overall Department of Defense (DoD) reserve recruiting goals, the DoD and four of the six components met their overall reserve recruiting objectives in FY 2000 (see Figure 2.1).

Figure 2.1
Percentage of Reserve Recruiting Objective Achieved in FY 2000, by Component

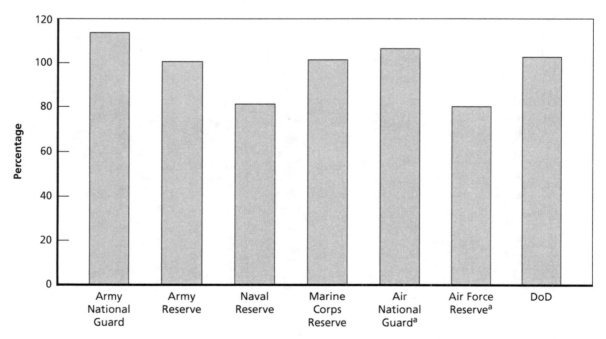

SOURCE: Based on data sent to the authors from Accession Policy, Office of the Under Secretary of Defense for Personnel and Readiness.

[a]The Air National Guard and the Air Force Reserve recruit to fill local unit vacancies and have no monthly goals.

RAND *MG202-2.1*

The overall recruiting performance is a combination of recruiting outcomes for PS and NPS accessions. In FY 2000, 55 percent of reserve accessions were previously in the service. The fraction of PS recruits among accessions in each of the six reserve components varies from a low of 38 percent in the U.S. Marine Corps Reserve to 82 percent in the Naval Reserve (U.S. Department of Defense, 2001). In part reflecting the differing sources of recruits, the components use different approaches to generate recruiting goals. For example, the Air National Guard and the Air Force Reserve recruit to fill local unit vacancies rather than establishing monthly goals. The Naval Reserve sets only a PS goal, while the Air Force Reserve establishes only an overall goal.

While the percentage of the DoD reserve recruiting goal declined from FY 1997 through FY 1999 for both PS and NPS accessions, the decline was more substantial for PS recruiting. The DoD did meet its reserve recruiting objectives for FY 2000, but this was achieved by exceeding its NPS mission, which made up for a shortfall in PS recruiting, in which DoD recruited only 90 percent of its goal, also called its "mission" (see Figures 2.1–2.3). As the figures show, in FY 2000 four components had problems meeting their PS mission, while all the components met their NPS mission.

The active components also recruit NPS individuals and may serve as a source of competition with the reserves for these recruits. Active duty NPS recruiting has been difficult in recent years. In FY 1999, the Army missed its recruiting mission, as did the Air Force, the service long regarded as being immune to recruiting difficulties. While all the services

Figure 2.2
Percentage of Reserve PS Recruiting Objective Achieved in FY 2000, by Component

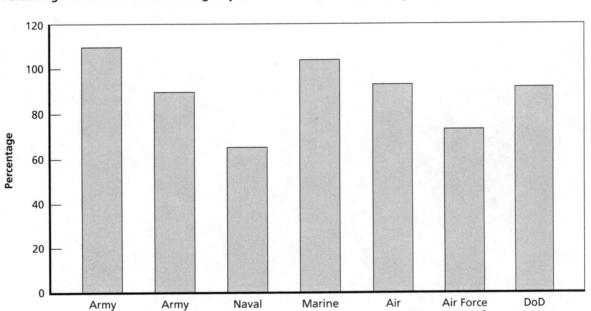

SOURCE: Based on data sent to the authors from Accession Policy, Office of the Under Secretary of Defense for Personnel and Readiness.
aThe Air Force recruits to reach only an overall goal.
RAND MG202-2.2

Figure 2.3
Percentage of Reserve NPS Recruiting Objective Achieved in FY 2000, by Component

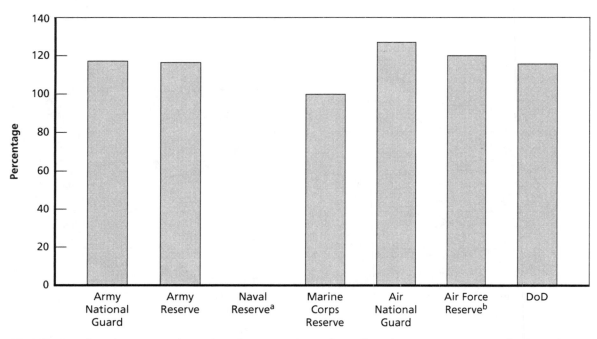

SOURCE: Based on data sent to the authors from Accession Policy, Office of the Under Secretary of Defense for Personnel and Readiness.
[a]The Naval Reserve establishes only a PS goal.
[b]The Air Force recruits to reach only an overall goal.
RAND *MG202-2.3*

achieved their missions in FY 2000, the percentage of recruits who were high quality[1] declined to its lowest level in more than a decade (see Figure 2.4).

In contrast, the quality of NPS reserve recruits largely stayed constant over the decade (see Figures 2.5 and 2.6). Between FY 1992 and FY 2000, the percentage of NPS reserve recruits with a high school diploma averaged between 87 percent and 91 percent (see Figure 2.5). Similarly, over the same period the percentage of NPS reserve recruits scoring in AFQT categories I–IIIA stayed in a narrow range—between 64 and 69 percent (see Figure 2.6).

Demographic Characteristics of Recruits

Another important aspect of the recruiting context is the demographic makeup of recruits. Demographic characteristics inform researchers on what types of civilian factors need to be incorporated into a model of recruiting. For example, if recruits came largely from the elderly population, it would imply different factors for the model than would be warranted if re-

---

[1] High-quality recruits are those who completed high school and scored in the upper 50 percent on the Armed Forces Qualification Test (AFQT).

Figure 2.4
Percentage of High-Quality NPS Active Duty Recruits, by Fiscal Year

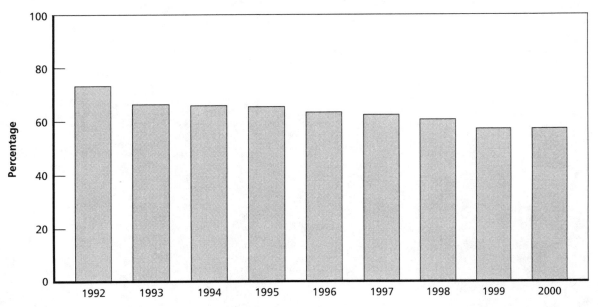

SOURCE: Based on data sent to the authors from Accession Policy, Office of the Under Secretary of Defense for Personnel and Readiness.
RAND *MG202-2.4*

Figure 2.5
Percentage of NPS Reserve Recruits with High School Diplomas, by Fiscal Year

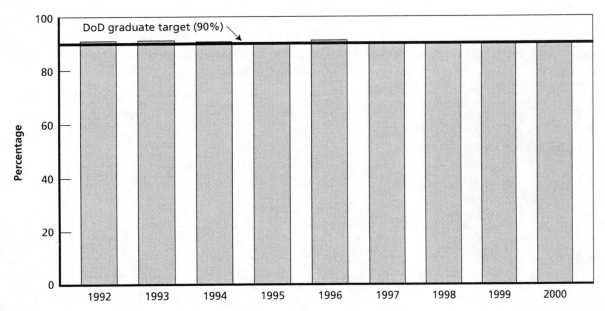

SOURCE: Based on data sent to the authors from Accession Policy, Office of the Under Secretary of Defense for Personnel and Readiness.
RAND *MG202-2.5*

Figure 2.6
Percentage of NPS Reserve Recruits Scoring in AFQT Categories I–IIIA, by Fiscal Year

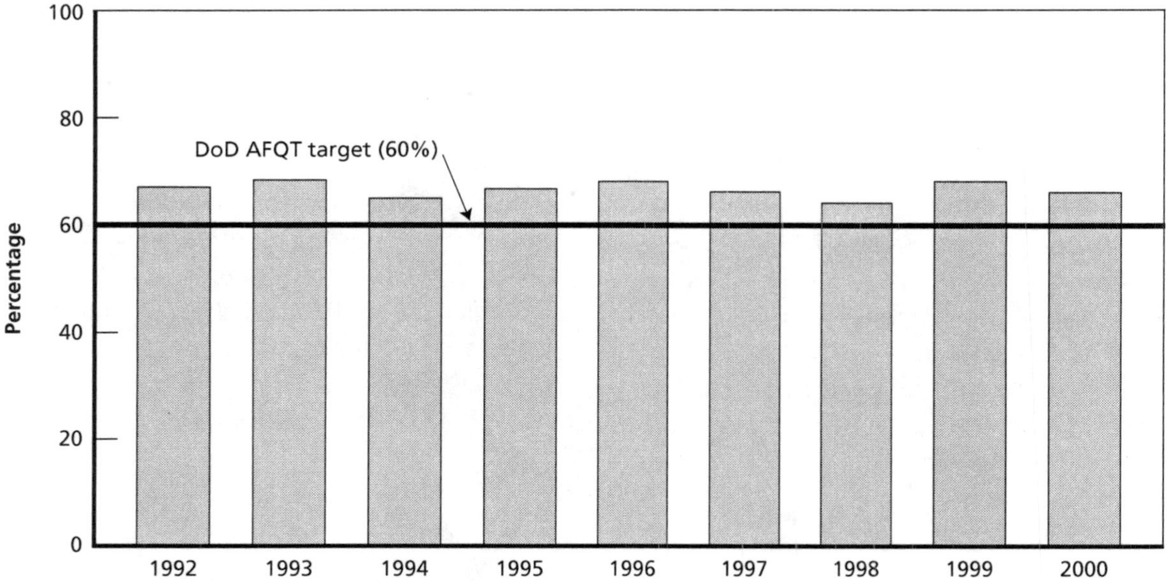

SOURCE: Based on data sent to the authors from Accession Policy, Office of the Under Secretary of Defense for Personnel and Readiness.
RAND MG202-2.6

cruits were drawn from the youth population. While the companion report of this project (Kilburn et al. unpublished) describes recruit demographics in detail, we briefly review some of the key recruit attributes here.

The primary demographic characteristics related to recruiting are age, race/ethnicity, and gender. Like for the active force, the bulk of reserve recruits come from the 17 to 24 age group. However, many more reserve recruits are older than 24, compared with active duty recruits. In FY 1999, only about 7 percent of NPS active force recruits were older than 24. In contrast, about 14 percent of NPS reserve recruits were over age 24 in FY 1999 (U.S. Department of Defense, 2003). The fraction of PS reserve recruits who are over 24 is larger—over two-thirds (U.S. Department of Defense, 2003). The age distribution of reserve accessions has remained relatively stable over the last decade.

During the All-Volunteer Force era, minorities—individuals who are black, Hispanic, or of some other non-white race or ethnicity—have been overrepresented among active duty recruits, compared with their civilian representation. However, the difference has narrowed in more recent years. In FY 2001 minorities made up 37 percent of NPS active duty recruits, compared with 35 percent of civilians aged 18 to 24 (U.S. Department of Defense, 2003). The overrepresentation of minorities among active duty recruits is primarily driven by the overrepresentation of black recruits. While 14 percent of the 18- to 24-year-old civilian population were black, this population accounted for nearly 20 percent of new active duty recruits. Hispanics were actually underrepresented among recruits (11 percent of recruits, compared with almost 16 percent of the youth population), and the category "other" has had about the same representation among active duty recruits and the youth population (6 percent of recruits versus 5 percent of youth). Minority representation increased steadily over the 1990s, rising from 27 percent of new recruits in FY 1991 to 37 percent in FY 1999.

Over the same period, minorities as a fraction of the 18- to 24-year-old population grew from about 29 percent to 35 percent.

Minorities were slightly underrepresented in the ranks of NPS reserve accessions in FY 2001: Only 29 percent were minorities (U.S. Department of Defense, 2003). Unlike the pattern for active duty recruits, the representation of racial and ethnic groups among reserve recruits has remained relatively constant over the 1990s.

The gender composition of reserve accessions has been the only demographic characteristic that changed markedly among reserve recruits over the 1990s. Toward the beginning of the 1990s, fewer than 15 percent of accessions were women. By FY 2001, nearly 20 percent of reserve accessions were women. Not surprisingly, a higher fraction of NPS reserve recruits are female. About 25 percent of NPS accessions were women in FY 1999, compared with 17 percent of PS accessions. A slightly smaller fraction of active duty recruits in FY 1999 were female—18 percent (U.S. Department of Defense, 2003). This number represents an increase over the decade from about 13 percent in FY 1991.

Trends That Would Be Likely to Influence Recruiting

Lastly, we review trends in contextual factors that would be likely to affect reserve recruiting. Again, these are discussed in more detail in the companion report (Kilburn et al., unpublished). Here we briefly summarize those factors that are included in the empirical model discussed in this monograph.

Changing Economy

The 1990s experienced a long post-war economic expansion accompanied by unprecedented growth in the stock market. By early 2001, however, growth rates sagged, and by the middle of the year, a recession was under way. The strong economy hurt recruiting in the 1990s, but the more recent weakening of the economy is likely to benefit active duty and reserve recruiting.

Changes in Firm Size

Data from the Current Population Survey (CPS) do not show any significant trend in the distribution of the size of firms in which people work. The perception is that larger firms would be better able to accommodate workers who were called away on reserve duty and, hence, that workers in large firms would be more likely to enlist in the reserves. However, it is well-documented that larger firms tend to pay higher wages (Schmidt and Zimmermann, 1991). If workers in larger firms earn higher wages, they may be less likely to enlist in the reserves for financial reasons. On net, it is unclear which of these two effects would dominate.

The Time Use of Men with Families

A sphere that is increasingly demanding more time from men in the age group of reserve recruits is family life. The total time fathers spend with their children has grown from about 19 hours a week in 1965 to approximately 29 hours a week in 1998 (Bianchi, 2000). In addition, data show that men are also spending significantly more time contributing to other areas of home life than they did in previous decades (Juster and Stafford, 1991; South and

Spitz, 1994). With more household activities and greater responsibilities, family men may have less time for a second job such as the reserves.

Rising Attendance and Cost of College

Another set of important demographic trends over the 1990s was related to college attendance. Record numbers of recent high school graduates have been enrolling in college at the same time that college costs have risen faster than the rate of inflation (see Asch, Kilburn, and Klerman, 1999). Why would college attendance be rising at the same time that college was becoming so much more expensive? The explanation is largely because the returns on college education—the earnings premium that college graduates receive above the earnings of high school graduates—have grown. In 1979, this premium was 27 percent, and by 1997, it was 44 percent (Mishel, Bernstein, and Schmitt, 1999). With more people attending college, fewer may enter the reserves.

Smaller Veteran Population

As the size of the armed forces declined over the 1990s, there was a concomitant decline in the veteran population. In calendar year 1992, nearly 16 percent of adults age 30 to 64 were veterans. By 1999, this percentage had shrunk to approximately 12 percent (see Figure 2.7). This has the potential to hurt reserve recruiting (as well as active duty recruiting) because there are fewer veteran role models for youth to follow.

Shrinking Prior-Service Pool

The majority of accessions into the reserves come from those with previous active duty service. Most (95 percent) are individuals who exited active duty during the current fiscal year

Figure 2.7
Percentage of Adult Population Who Are Veterans, by Calendar Year

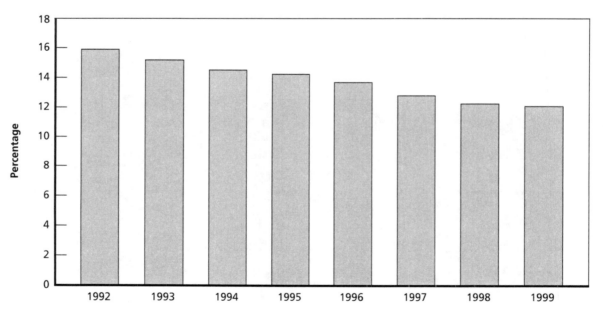

SOURCE: U.S. Census Bureau, 1992–2002.
RAND MG202-2.7

or the previous one. Thus, with a smaller military force due to the 1990s drawdown, there are fewer people exiting from active duty and a smaller pool of potential PS entrants. Figure 2.8 shows the trend in the number of active duty exits by fiscal year. While this effect may be partially offset with a greater pool of people in the NPS population with an inclination to join the military, it does raise concerns for future recruiting into the reserves.

State Guard Educational Incentives

Some states offer tuition deferments at state colleges and universities to State Guard accessions. The other components and active duty recruiters have viewed this benefit as a potent source of competition. Over half of the states offered full or partial tuition deferments over the decade. There was little change in the number of states offering educational incentives however: In 1992, 30 states offered tuition benefits to State Guard recruits, and in 1999, 33 states offered such benefits. In addition to tuition deferments, some states provided other types of educational benefits to State Guard recruits, such as forgiving loans. The incidence of these types of benefits was relatively low, with 12 to 14 states offering such benefits in each year between 1992 and 1999.[2]

Now that we have reviewed recent trends in reserve and active recruiting and factors that might be expected to influence recruiting, we turn to a review of the literature on estimating enlistment models.

Figure 2.8
Number of Active Duty Exits, by Fiscal Year

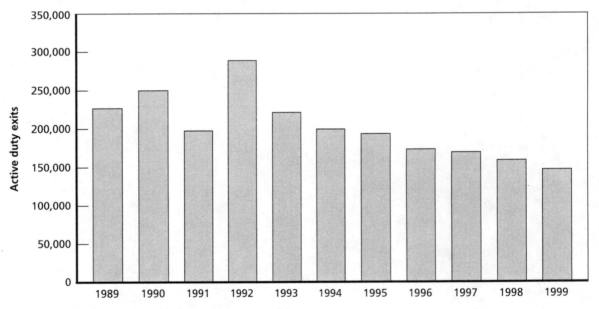

SOURCE: U.S. Department of Defense, various years (b).
RAND MG202-2.8

---

[2] These numbers are based on data reported in Smith and Gordon, various years.

CHAPTER THREE

Previous Literature

This chapter describes the reserve and active duty recruit supply models that have been estimated in the literature. We describe different objectives these models may have, the theoretical foundations of the models, and the empirical strategy for estimating these models. Here we provide a concise review of recruit supply models, highlighting the information policymakers can glean from the estimates and the way these models could be improved. We review what information these types of models can produce. We also enumerate some weaknesses in the existing estimates of recruit supply models and propose some strategies to overcome these shortcomings. In addition, we discuss generic recruit supply models, in that we do not distinguish between active duty and reserve models.

The Objectives of Recruit Supply Models

For several decades, a staple of recruiting research has been estimates of "recruit supply models." These models typically attempt to explain recruiting outcomes, like the number of high-quality accessions, as a function of labor market and recruiting policy variables.

In their simplest form, recruit supply models take the following form:

$$Y_{tg} = \beta_1' X_{1tg} + \beta_2' X_{2tg} + \varepsilon ,$$

where Y_{tg} is the number of high-quality recruits who accessed in time period t in geographic area g, X_{1tg} is a vector of demographic and labor market variables at time t in geographic area g, and X_{2tg} is a vector of recruiting policy variables at time t in geographic area g. The coefficient β_1' represents the effects of demographic and labor market variables, X_{1tg}. The coefficient β_2' represents the effectiveness of the recruiting policy variables, X_{2tg}. For this discussion, we are assuming that the model will be linear. Given this basic form, recruit supply models could be used to provide two types of information, which we will call *prediction* and *policy variable effectiveness*.

If prediction is the objective of an estimation exercise, the goal is to estimate a model that will generate a predicted outcome variable that most closely resembles actual outcomes. This model will produce predictions of the number of recruits that would be expected in a given time period and geographic area based on the demographic and economic variables and recruiting policy variables in that time period and geographic area. The predicted value from the appropriate model, denoted and calculated as

$$\hat{Y}_{tg} = \hat{\beta}_1 X_{1tg} + \hat{\beta}_2 X_{2tg},$$

should be unbiased, such that $E(Y_{tg} - \hat{Y}_{tg}) = E(e_{tg}) = 0$.

In other words, this model is chosen so that the predicted value for Y_{tg} most closely approximates the actual value of recruiting outcomes, Y_{tg}. Several measures have been proposed to measure the predictive power of the model. Measures such as the root mean-squared error, R^2, adjusted R^2, and Theil's U statistic are based on squared residuals obtained from the estimated model. For more information on this topic, see Efron (1978), Greene (2000), Theil (1961), and Ellis et al. (1996).

If prediction is the objective of the model, the characteristics of the coefficient estimates are not the key criteria for selecting the model. This implies that it may be of little consequence if the model produces biased coefficient estimates or coefficient estimates that are not minimum variance. The practical implication of developing a model based solely on predictive power is that the coefficient estimates produced by these models should not be used to inform policy.

A second objective of recruit supply models has been to estimate recruit policy variable effectiveness and the effects of economic, demographic, and other dynamic factors. In terms of the specification above, this means to estimate values of β (i.e., β_1 and β_2), which will indicate how changing the recruiting policy variables (the X_{2tg}) or how changes in other factors such as the economy (in X_{1tg}) would affect the number of additional recruits accessed. In this case, traditionally the model selected would be the one that produces:

1. *Unbiased estimates of the coefficients.* This implies that the coefficient estimate is equal to the true estimate, or $E(\hat{\beta} - \beta) = 0$.

2. *Minimum variance estimates.* This implies that the sampling variance of the estimate of $\hat{\beta}$ is smaller than the sampling variation produced by any other estimator (see Greene, 2000).

When the objective of the model is to understand policy effectiveness, the model selected is the one that elicits the desirable properties of the coefficient estimates. In this case, the model is not selected based on its qualities of the prediction. The practical implication is that using a model that was developed to examine the effectiveness of policy options may not be the best model for prediction.

The objective of the estimation exercise guides not only the way the optimal model is selected but also the variables selected to appear as explanatory factors. If the objective is prediction, then the strategy would be to include as many relevant variables as possible, including potentially endogenous[1] variables. However, if the objective of the model is to learn how

---

[1] Endogenous variables are those that are explained by other variables in the model. In contrast, exogenous variables are not related to the model and are determined independently of the variables in the model.

effective certain policy instruments are or what factors could lead to recruiting problems in the future, then it is necessary to be more selective about which variables to include. For example, if we wanted to determine how recruiting would change with changes in the unemployment rate, holding other things constant, then we would not include other indicators of the economy that would be highly correlated with the unemployment rate, such as average hours worked. If we were to include such variables, then part of the effect of the unemployment rate could be captured by the other economic variables.

Most of the recruit supply literature has focused on understanding policy effectiveness as its primary objective. As a result, the literature has generally estimated models that yield desirable properties of the coefficient estimates rather than generating optimal predictions. In addition, the literature has generally been selective about what variables to include as explanatory variables so that the interpretation of coefficients for individual variables would be straightforward. Similar to most of the previous recruiting studies, our primary objective in this analysis is to identify the demographic, labor market, and policy variables that affect reserve recruiting. This information should then be able to be used by policymakers to predict what changes in the economy or in demographics or which other factors may lead to recruiting shortfalls in the future.

Theoretical Foundations of Recruit Supply Models

We now describe the theoretical models that form the underpinning for economic studies of reserve and active duty recruiting. We begin by discussing the "moonlighting model," which has been used to model the decision to enter the reserves. We then outline the individual enlistment decision model, which has been used to characterize the active duty enlistment decision.

Reserve Enlistment: The Moonlighting Model

An economic model of individual decisionmaking known as the moonlighting model underlies many estimates of aggregate reserve recruiting outcomes. This model is a standard in the labor economics literature (Shishko and Rostker, 1976), whereby members of a household decide whether to take on a second job—to moonlight—in addition to their primary job. The basic decision rule a potential reserve recruit faces in this model is whether to spend time moonlighting in the reserves versus other potential uses of that time, such as spending more time at the primary job, moonlighting at some other job, or using the time for leisure. Note that in the parlance of this economic model, "leisure" refers to all non-labor-force activities and hence may include such home-based responsibilities as caring for children and home maintenance as well as more relaxing pursuits.

Grissmer, Kirby, and Sze (1992) argue that the decision of whether to participate in the reserves is not a direct application of the moonlighting model. They contend that the extensive training required for the reserves (having an effect on the time costs and the training benefits of participation), the priority their reserve participation can take over their primary job, the job security of the reserves, and many of the nonmonetary benefits of participating all serve to make the decision to participate in the reserves much more complex than the decision of whether to moonlight beyond one's primary job. Nevertheless, the decision comes down to the same basic terms: An individual joins the reserves if the monetary and nonmonetary value of being in the reserves exceeds that of all other potential uses of that time. This is the basic theory underlying the models we use in this analysis.

Studies have identified several types of factors that are related to individuals' decisions to join or stay in the reserves (see Asch, 1993; Grissmer, Kirby, and Sze, 1992; and Kirby and Naftel, 1998). These factors are often grouped into two categories: supply factors and demand factors. Supply factors generally reflect the relative value of alternative ways an individual could spend time that would have been used for reserve participation. One such set of factors is related to the value of the person's leisure time, or time spent at home. These factors include whether the person is married and has children, because the value to the household of the person spending time at home is higher when there are children to care for and when there are other members of the household. Moreover, family members' attitudes toward reserve duty also play a role in the individual's decision to join the reserves (Grissmer, Kirby, and Sze, 1992).

Another set of supply factors includes characteristics of the person's primary job. Whether the primary job is in the government sector, in the private sector, or is self-employment has a bearing on the decision to participate in the reserves. Government employees are more likely to join the reserves, and self-employed workers are less likely to join the reserves. These patterns are probably related to the relative generosity of government reserve benefit policies (see Kilburn et al., unpublished). Working long hours on the primary job is also associated with a lower probability of joining the reserves (see Marquis and Kirby, 1989). The attitudes and policies of a person's primary civilian employer toward reserve service are also likely to influence an individual's participation (Grissmer, Kirby, and Sze, 1992).

Lastly, other supply factors that have a bearing on whether someone chooses to enlist in the reserves are the characteristics of alternative civilian moonlighting opportunities. In a strong labor market, second jobs in the civilian sector will appear relatively more attractive than in weaker labor markets, reflecting higher wage opportunities, more job openings, and a higher probability of finding a second job in the civilian sector.

In addition to these supply factors, which characterize the potential recruits' other opportunities, a set of demand factors that characterize reserve opportunities also affect potential reservists' decisions regarding enlistment (Asch, 1993). These demand factors can be influenced and set by the services and the various recruiting commands, based on the relative demand for recruits. For example, reserve policies such as compensation, health care coverage, training, and reenlistment incentives (such as bonuses) will affect the relative value of reserve participation to the individual. The perceived likelihood of mobilization and the potential risks of reserve duty will also play a role. Empirical studies have found that deployments—especially nonhostile deployments—raise retention among active duty service members. Hosek and Totten (2002) report that among enlisted active duty service members, those who deployed had higher reenlistment relative to those who did not deploy. Reenlistment was higher for those with more nonhostile deployments and changed little for those with hostile deployments. In a study of officer retention, Fricker (2002) finds that for junior and midgrade active duty officers, more deployment was associated with greater retention. Junior officers who experienced hostile deployments were less likely to be retained than their peers who experienced nonhostile deployments but still more likely to be retained than those who had not been deployed. Studies also have recognized that recruiter behavior plays a role in recruiting outcomes and hence include policies representing recruiter incentive plans or recruiter effort in the model (see Dertouzos, 1985).

Theory Behind Recruiting Models

The model underlying individual decisions to enlist in the military is very similar to the moonlighting model. Earlier economic models of individual enlistment decisions (Hosek and Peterson 1985; Hosek, Peterson, and Eden, 1986; Kilburn and Klerman, 1999; Kilburn, 1994; Kim et al., 1980) are variants of the random utility model (McFadden, 1983).

The individual who is deciding whether or not to enlist is eligible for military enlistment and can choose between enlistment and other activities such as college, employment, and working in the home. By assumption, in the basic random utility framework, individuals choose the activity that yields the highest expected utility. An individual chooses to enlist in the military if the utility of enlisting is greater than the utility of the other alternatives, or

$$U_{im} > U_{ij} \text{ for } j = 1, 2, \ldots J,$$

where U indicates utility, i represents the individual, m represents the military, and j represents nonmilitary alternatives.

This behavioral model is translated into a statistical model by expressing the likelihood that an individual makes the observed choice as a probability. The probability that an individual chooses to enlist over some other activity, j, is

$$\Pr(U_{im} > U_{ij}).$$

Let the approximate utility to individual i of alternative k be a function of characteristics of the individual X_i and a random error component ε_{ik} such that

$$U_{ik} = f_k(X_i) + \varepsilon_{ik}.$$

The X_i includes such characteristics as the resources the individual's family has for funding educational investments, the person's AFQT score, and other characteristics that would be expected to alter the relative utility of the competing alternatives. Models of occupational or educational choice typically specify the utility of the alternatives as a function of potential wages, investment cost, earnings growth, or returns to investment (see, for example, Manski and Wise, 1983; Willis and Rosen, 1979; and Hosek and Peterson, 1985).

Estimating Reserve Recruiting Models

The theoretical model of individual enlistment decisions serves as the foundation for two empirical approaches to estimating enlistment models. The most common empirical approach to estimating enlistment models uses aggregate-level data to understand how market-level factors influence recruiting outcomes at the level of a geographic unit, such as a state or recruiting station territory. This approach takes aggregate-level outcomes as the summing up of the individual decisions outlined above across many individuals. In these empirical estimates, the outcome of interest is the number of recruits who enlisted in a particular geographic area in a specified period of time instead of whether a particular individual enlisted. Explanatory variables include measures of the supply and demand factors enumerated above, at the level of the geographic unit. These estimates produce information about how the number of recruits responds to changes in aggregate variables such as the number of recruiters, the unemployment rate, or civilian pay relative to military pay.

Aggregate-level models have most often been used to estimate recruit supply for the active force (Murray and McDonald, 1999; Polich, Dertouzos, and Press, 1986). Murray and McDonald (1999) specify the supply of high-quality recruits in a time period in a geographic unit as

$$H = \gamma_1 D + \gamma_2 S + \gamma_3 X_H + \gamma_4 E_H + \varepsilon_H, \tag{1}$$

where H is the number of high-quality recruits in a geographic area, D is a vector of dummy variables representing time periods, S is a vector of dummy variables representing the geographic units, and X_H is a vector containing the variables that influence supply. These include a representative civilian wage, measures of military compensation, unemployment rates, size of the youth population, measures of military recruiting advertising in the area, and indicators for enlistment incentive programs available, such as bonuses or educational incentives. The variable E_H represents recruiter effort and ε_H is an error term.

Since recruiter effort is unobservable, another equation is specified for recruiter effort. Murray and McDonald (1999) use the following specification for recruiter effort:

$$E_H = \tau_1 + \tau_2 X_E + \tau_3 M_H + \tau_4 M_L + \tau_5 P_H + \tau_6 P_L + \tau_7 R + \varepsilon_1. \tag{2}$$

The vector X_E contains factors that influence recruiters' choice of effort. Murray and McDonald include the same variables in vector X_H above for the vector X_E. The variables M_H and M_L are the high- and low-quality recruiting goals for a geographic area in a particular time period, and P_H and P_L are the area's recruiters' performance relative to goals in the previous month. R represents the total number of recruiters and ε_1 represents an error term.

Substituting (2), which is a function of observable variables, into (1) for the unobserved effort yields an estimable equation for high-quality recruits:

$$H = \beta_1 + \gamma_1 D + \gamma_2 S + \gamma_3 X_H + \beta_2 X_E + \beta_3 M_H + \beta_4 M_L + \beta_5 P_H + \beta_6 P_L + \beta_7 R + \mu_H.$$

Studies that estimate aggregate reserve recruit supply generally use the same framework as studies that examine aggregate active duty supply (Warner and Asch, 1995). The results of the reserve recruit supply studies are also very similar to the active duty results (Tan, 1991; Kostiuk and Grogan, 1987; and Marquis and Kirby, 1989). In general, this literature finds significant relationships between a number of key policy and labor market variables—in particular, military pay, unemployment rates, and the number of recruiters—and recruiting outcomes.

The second approach to estimating enlistment models uses individual-level observations rather than aggregate-level observations as the units of analysis. These estimates reflect the probabilities that individuals choose to enlist based on their characteristics and features of their alternative choices, as discussed above. These estimates indicate how individual-level factors, such as a person's college prospects or labor market opportunities, influence individuals' decisions to enlist instead of work in the labor force or attend college, for instance (see Kilburn and Klerman, 1999). While this approach has not been used to understand reserve recruiting, the reserve retention literature (for instance, Marquis and Kirby, 1989; Grissmer, Kirby, and Sze, 1992) usually uses this empirical strategy.

The empirical specification for these models derives from rewriting equation (1) in terms of the observed characteristics of the individual and in terms of the error component, producing the following expression for the probability that the individual chooses to enlist in the military, m:

$$\Pr\left(\left[f_m(Z_i) + \varepsilon_{im}\right] > \left[f_j(Z_i) + \varepsilon_{ij}\right]\right) \text{ for all } j,$$

where the vector, Z, incorporates all factors in D, S, X_H, and E_H.

Assuming a linear form for the function $f_k(X_i)$ and an extreme value distribution for the error yields the multinomial logit model (McFadden, 1973):

$$\Pr(k = m) = \frac{e^{b'_m X_i}}{\sum_k e^{b'_k X_i}}.$$

This model expresses the probability that the individual chooses choice m as a function of the characteristics of the individual and the attributes of the choices. The estimates of interest will be coefficient values, β, and their significance levels.

The probability that each individual enlists rises as the coefficients on the individual characteristics and choice attributes are higher for enlistment than other alternatives, provided that the variables are all positive. In terms of the equation above, this is equivalent to saying that the probability that an individual enlists is higher when $\beta_m > \beta_k$.

Individual characteristics influence the probability that one person enlists relative to another person. One person will be more likely to enlist than another person if that individual has characteristics that tend to raise the utility of enlisting relative to other alternatives, or the probability of enlisting rises as the military alternative has attributes that raise the utility of enlisting relative to the other alternatives. For example, if a particular individual characteristic, say X_{i1}, raises the probability of enlisting more than that of choosing the alternatives $(\beta_{m1} > \beta_{k1})$, then people with higher levels of X_{i1} will be more likely to enlist than people with lower levels of X_{i1}.

Summary of the Literature Review

Our discussion about the objectives of recruit supply models indicate that models of recruit supply can be used for at least two different purposes and that the model selected for a particular study reflects the objective of the study. As a result, models developed to assess the effectiveness of policy variables are not necessarily the optimal models for prediction, and vice versa. In this monograph, we are interested in identifying the relationships between economic, demographic, and policy variables and recruiting outcomes, so we use the most common approach to selecting a model, which yields optimal properties of the coefficient estimates.

We have discussed the theoretical and empirical approaches the literature has used in estimating active duty and reserve recruit supply models. In the next chapter, we outline our approach to estimating enlistment models.

CHAPTER FOUR

Our Approach to Estimating an Enlistment Model

We estimate a model of reserve enlistment that departs from the previous literature in several ways. First, we estimate two separate models, one for NPS accessions and another for PS accessions. We separate NPS accessions from PS accessions because there are likely to be different decision processes that come into play for the two groups. In addition, NPS potential recruits have an alternative to joining the reserves that is rarely a consideration for PS potential recruits: active duty enlistment. Second, we include both reserve and active duty enlistment as choice alternatives for NPS individuals. Third, the specification we estimate for NPS accessions is the grouped multinomial logit model, which incorporates features of both the individual enlistment specification and the aggregate-level specification described above.

The unit of observation in our NPS and PS models will be a state FY. We choose states as the unit of analysis, as opposed to recruiting station or some other geographic unit, because information on home states is available for nearly all personnel. Furthermore, most of the explanatory variables can be computed easily across states, but not across other geographic areas.

Non-Prior-Service Model

We assume that an individual without prior military experience chooses between:

1. entering active duty
2. entering the reserves
3. not enlisting in the military.

Note that individuals who choose (2) or (3) are likely to attend school, work, or engage in activities at home as part of that choice. Those who enlist in active duty generally engage in home activities as well, but are much less likely to work at another job or attend school intensively at the same time. Most individuals facing these choices are very young—generally 20 years old or younger—and as a result, they are unlikely to have strong labor force attachment. Given this characterization for NPS individuals, these choices are not well described by the moonlighting theory.

An advantage to including active duty as a separate choice in a model of NPS enlistment is that it could help elucidate some of the tradeoffs between active duty and reserve enlistment. For example, it could turn out that a higher unemployment rate leads to fewer reserve accessions because it could induce many people who would have entered the civilian workforce and the reserves to enter active duty instead. While other research has estimated multiple-choice models of active duty enlistment (compared with the choice of working or college attendance, Kilburn and Klerman, 1999), this is the first time we are aware of that active duty and reserve enlistment are included as alternative choices.

We use the random utility framework outlined in the previous chapter to characterize an individual's choice between active duty enlistment, reserve enlistment, and no enlistment. However, because we do not have data on the choice of each individual and their characteristics, we estimate a *grouped multinomial logit model*. This specification combines observations on individuals in a state at a point in time and uses the fraction of individuals from that state who make each choice as the dependent variable.[1] Our dependent variables are:

1. the fraction of eligible high-quality young people who enlist in active duty
2. the fraction of eligible high-quality young people who enlist in the reserves
3. the fraction of eligible high-quality young people who do not enlist in either active duty or reserves.

Specifically, we divide the number of active duty recruits and the number of reserve recruits in a state and year by the number of 18-year-olds (proxied by the number of 17-year-olds the year before) to obtain the first and second dependent variables, respectively. The third dependent variable is not estimated because it serves as the omitted "comparison" category in the multinomial logit estimation. While NPS recruits are typically ages 17 to 24, using one age (in our case, 18) sets the denominator on the right scale and provides a reasonable proxy for the number of eligible NPS recruits. We discuss the rationale for this in greater detail in Appendix B. We use states as the geographic areas because most of the explanatory variables cannot be grouped by narrower geographic areas such as recruiting stations. Furthermore, having narrower geographic areas would produce more sampling errors in the explanatory variables. The model is weighted by our proxy for the number of 18-year-olds in a state in a given year. Detailed information about the data sources and variable creation is provided in Appendix B.

How a variable affects active duty and reserve recruiting would depend on whether the activity that variable directly affects is a complement or a substitute to active duty and reserve recruiting. For example, attending college would be a substitute to enlisting in active duty, but it could be a substitute or complement to participating in the reserves. Thus, an increase in college tuition should increase active duty recruiting but would have an uncertain effect on reserve recruiting. In this case, reserve recruiting might be higher among those who consider college and the reserves to be substitutes, but reserve recruiting may be lower among some of the reserves' potential recruits who were going to attend college as their primary activity and now would turn to active duty. We would expect the same uncertainty for variables that directly affect the utility associated with being in the labor force. For example, a decrease in the unemployment rate could draw potential active duty recruits to enter the civilian labor force instead, which increases the pool of people who may enlist in the reserves. At the same time, the better job opportunities would provide better second job options, thereby reducing participation in the reserves.

---

[1] This type of dependent variable is somewhat similar to that used in Cotterman (1986), which was the number of enlistment contracts signed for each active duty service in a state and year, divided by the population of 17- to 21-year-old males in the state. He uses generalized least squares to estimate the model.

Explanatory Variables Included in the Model

The explanatory variables included in the model are factors that influence the relative utility of the alternative choices to individuals. We include the variables that have typically been included in recruiting models in the literature, but we also add some novel variables as well.

Economic Variables. One of the most common factors included in recruiting models is a measure of the well-being of the economy. This represents the availability of job opportunities in the civilian sector, one of the primary alternatives to joining active duty. Thus, the health of the economy would raise the utility of entering the labor force. We would expect that with a stronger economy, fewer would enter active duty because of the better job opportunities in the civilian sector. For reserve accessions, however, the direction of the effect is not as clear. A stronger economy would produce more opportunities for second jobs, which could reduce the number of people inclined to enter the reserves. But, at the same time, some of the people who were inclined to enter active duty but instead took advantage of a good civilian job offer resulting from the strong economy may enter the reserves (since they had some taste for military life) so that they could still experience the military. Therefore, the pool of potential reserve entrants would be larger.

Nearly every previous recruiting study we reviewed included the unemployment rate as an indicator of the strength of the economy. We include the annual state unemployment rates (adjusted to match DoD fiscal years). Wages are also representative of the value of civilian labor market opportunities. We include median wages for men with just a high school diploma and median wages for men with four years of college and no more. We include both of these measures because there has been an increasing premium of college-graduate wages over high-school-graduate wages in the last decade (see Mishel, Bernstein, and Schmitt, 1999), and the employment opportunities for college graduates compared with those for high school graduates at the local level are likely to influence the decision to attend college. While the unemployment rate and wages are likely to be correlated, we found that our estimates of the unemployment rate coefficients did not vary substantially when we excluded wages.

Educational Opportunities. College attendance is increasingly a source of competition for recruits (Asch, Kilburn, and Klerman, 1999; Kilburn and Klerman, 1999). To characterize the relative value of attending college, we include variables that capture the cost of and return on college attendance. One of these, wages for college graduates, was discussed above. To proxy for the costs of college in a state, we also include the average in-state tuition for public colleges in the state and year. Another variable we include is an indicator variable for the availability of a merit-based scholarship program in the state. Georgia implemented the first of these within-state merit-based programs when it offered the HOPE scholarship starting in 1994, and other states have followed suit with variants of this program.[2] These programs would likely reduce the number of accessions into both active duty and the reserves in the states with these programs. We created a dummy variable, for which a state-FY obser-

---

[2] The HOPE program uses state lottery funds to finance free tuition at public colleges, fees, and book allowances for all graduates of a Georgia high school with at least a B average in high school. Other states have followed with similar programs, but they vary in the comprehensiveness of the program and the amount of assistance provided. For example, Florida requires a combined score of 1180 on the Scholastic Aptitude Test, and Kentucky offers only a $2,500 scholarship for eligible students. We code a state-FY observation as having a HOPE-like scholarship if it had very general eligibility criteria, it served a large number of students in the state, and it paid for at least tuition. This resulted in only four states with eligible programs, and 13 values of one for state-FY pairs in our data—(Florida, 1998–1999; Georgia, 1994–1999; Mississippi, 1996–1999; and South Carolina, 1999).

vation has a value of one if it had this type of scholarship. Factors that would increase the value of attending college would have a negative effect on active duty recruiting and an uncertain effect on reserve recruiting.

Demographic Factors. Other important influences on recruiting into the military are demographic factors, particularly race and ethnicity. Minorities are generally overrepresented in the military (Kilburn, 1994; U.S. Department of Defense, 2001), and hence we would expect higher enlistment rates in areas with large minority populations. We include the fraction of the population aged 17–24 who are black and the fraction who are Hispanic in our model.

Influencer Variables. In their estimates of individual enlistment decisions, Kilburn and Klerman (1999) found that having a parent in the military was one of the most important predictors of enlistment. Other research, such as Reville (1996), has also found that children are more likely to enter their parents' professions. Policymakers attribute a large role not only to parents, but also to other "influencers"—such as teachers, coaches, and other adults—in helping young people formulate their post-high-school plans. In recent years, the number of these influencers who have military experience has dropped dramatically, and there has been some concern that this will lead to having fewer influencers with a positive view toward military service. We include, as a proxy for this factor, the fraction of the population in a state and year aged 25 to 65 who are veterans.

At the same time that the ranks of veterans in the population are shrinking, the fraction of the population with a college degree is rising (Asch, Kilburn, and Klerman, 1999). This rise in the number of those with a college degree is due in part to the growth in the college earnings premium over the last two decades. Like the patterns of occupational choice, children of college-educated individuals are much more likely to attend college themselves than children of people without a college degree. To account for this pattern, we also include the fraction of the 25- to 65-year-olds in the state and year with a college degree to account for differences in the number of influencers with college experience.

Civilian Workforce Characteristics. As discussed earlier, the characteristics of one's civilian job are likely to affect the likelihood of joining the reserves. Certain types of industries or employers have relatively more or less generous policies toward reserve participation. It appears that the government and larger firms have more flexible reserve policies (Kilburn et al., unpublished). Furthermore, the government sector is often perceived as being less susceptible to business cycle fluctuations, which would make civilian employment relatively more attractive. To account for these factors, we include a variable indicating the percentage of workers in a state who work for the government and the percentage of workers in different firm size categories. To our knowledge, no other recruiting estimates have included workforce characteristics.

Policy Variables. Most previous studies of recruiting have included policy variables such as the number of recruiters per capita, advertising, and bonus programs (for example, Cotterman, 1986; Polich, Dertouzos, and Press, 1986; Hosek, Peterson, and Eden, 1986). Given that our model is estimated at the state and year level, we can only include variables that vary across states and years and have data available across states and years. Thus, we cannot include enlistment bonuses because they are not specific to states, and we cannot use advertising expenses because they are not tracked consistently at the state level. We were able to obtain data on two such policy variables: the number of active duty recruiters and the availability of State Guard educational incentive programs. The number of recruiters has been included in numerous other recruiting estimates, but State Guard educational benefits has not been included. While we were able to obtain counts of active duty recruiters in states in each year, we were not able to obtain analogous counts of reserve recruiters. This inability to obtain such counts was due in part to the myriad ways that the components recruited, which led to inconsistent definitions of reserve recruiters across components and time, and also due to the fact that reserve data are not as well developed as active duty data. For the State Guard educational programs, we created dummy variables to indicate whether the state offered full or partial tuition deferments for in-state college students who signed up for the reserves.

We include both the number of active duty recruiters per 1,000 18-year-olds in the state FY and its square as explanatory variables. We expect that additional recruiters boost enlistment, but at a decreasing rate, which would imply a positive coefficient on the number of recruiters but a negative coefficient on its square. We also anticipate that the benefit from an additional active duty recruiter would be greater for active duty enlistments than for reserve enlistments. While we hypothesize that additional recruiters will always boost active duty recruiting, it could be the case that adding recruiters harms reserve enlistments if those additional recruits come at the expense of reserve recruiting. This depends on the degree to which active duty and reserve recruiting complement versus compete against each other.

Household Responsibility Indicators. Responsibilities in the household would be a competing use of time to joining the reserves, so that greater responsibilities would likely reduce the likelihood of joining the reserves. To capture household responsibilities, we create a variable indicating the percentage of 18- to 24-year-olds who are married with children.

State and Year Effects. We also include state and year dummy variables. The state variables capture state-specific effects that are not captured by the other variables in the model and do not vary over time. These are sometimes referred to as "unmeasured" or "unobserved" state effects. The year dummy variables account for trends in the propensity to enlist that are not accounted for by the model and may also reflect some of the "demand side" factors that change over time. Because we control for the year and state, we can interpret the estimates of the coefficients on the other variables as being the result of within-state changes over time (see Greene, 2000).

Prior-Service Model

The moonlighting model is more applicable to the decision to enlist for PS individuals. They are likely to be working a primary job and deciding how to spend their away-from-work hours. For the PS model, we examine only the decision of whether or not to enter the reserves. A person is assumed to enter the reserves if the monetary and nonmonetary value of being in the reserves exceeds that of all other potential uses of that time.

Ideally, we would estimate a similar probability model as we do for NPS accessions. Unfortunately, there is not a clearly defined approximation of eligible people who could become a PS accession to the reserves as there is for NPS accessions. The population could include people from a given state who left active duty in the last year or the last ten years. However, by using this approach, we cannot give the same probability of entering the reserves to people who left active duty or the reserves in the previous 12 months as we would to those who left the military ten years ago. Another challenge is that there is not a clearly defined approximation for the number of eligible PS reservists. Finally, if we did have an accurate count of the eligible PS individuals in a state, using that as the denominator in the dependent variable would be problematic. Explanatory variables such as the unemployment rate and college tuition would likely affect active duty retention as well as reserve recruiting. Hence, interpreting the results would be difficult for a specification with recruits in the numerator and those who have separated from service (separatees) in the denominator of the dependent variable—it would be difficult to gauge whether an estimated positive effect influenced the outcomes by increasing accessions or decreasing active duty attrition.

As a result, for the PS specification, we follow the literature and use the natural log of the actual number of PS accessions in a state FY as our dependent variable, and we estimate a linear regression model (Dertouzos, 1985; Polich, Dertouzos, and Press, 1986; Tan, 1991; and Murray and McDonald, 1999). We weight the observations by the number of enlisted personnel who exit active duty in the current and prior fiscal years. Our data indicate that of the PS accessions who had prior service in active duty as opposed to the reserve, 55 percent exited active duty the same fiscal year they accessed into the reserve, and 40 percent exited active duty in the prior fiscal year.

We expect that many of the same variables that affect the probability of entering active duty or the reserves for NPS individuals influence the probability of entering the reserves for those with prior service. Hence, we include the same set of factors in the PS specification that we included in the NPS specification. However, we expect that some of the effects may be different. For example, since these individuals already chose to participate in the military, we would think that the influence of the number of veterans in one's community or state would be less on the decision to enter the reserves for PS individuals than it would for those without prior service. Another example would be that the effects of tuition rates at public universities would have less of an effect because fewer PS individuals would consider college as an option than NPS individuals would.

For the PS specification, we change the set of covariates in three ways. First, we also include as regressors in the PS specification the number of people exiting active duty in the last few years who had ten years or less of active duty experience. Specifically, we include the number of exits from active duty from the current year, from the prior year, and from two and from three years prior to the relevant year. This should provide insight into how reserve recruiting fluctuates with the number of active duty exits. Second, we do not include the number of active duty recruiters, as we would expect this to have little bearing on PS reserve recruiting. Third, the variables for race and ethnicity represent the percentage of active duty exits in the fiscal year of the observation who were black or Hispanic rather than the percentage of 18-year-olds in these groups.

Empirical Challenges to Estimating Coefficients

There are several essential conditions required to estimate unbiased regression coefficients (see Greene, 2000). Two of them are likely to be in question for recruiting models:

1. None of the variables that explain the outcome also depend on the outcome.
2. There are no third variables that are correlated with both the explanatory variables and the outcome but that are not included in the model.[3]

---

[3] This is also known as having no omitted variables.

Including recruiting policy variables—such as the number of recruiters, advertising expenses, or enlistment bonuses—may violate the first condition, because policymakers may adjust these factors based on how successful the military services or reserve components are in recruiting. For example, if recruiting outcomes were particularly good in one state, policymakers might reallocate some of that state's recruiters to areas that were not doing so well. This might lead to the spurious result that reducing recruiters was associated with better recruiting outcomes.

Omitting policy variables, such as the number of recruiters, from the model could also be viewed as problematic if the number of recruiters was based in part on other factors included in the model. For example, another way to allocate recruiters might be to assign more recruiters to states with tougher recruiting environments due to robust economic conditions—i.e., more recruiters might be assigned to states with low unemployment rates. In this case, omitting the number of recruiters would violate the second condition above. The empirical consequence is that, if the number of recruiters was not included in the model, the coefficient estimates might erroneously suggest that low unemployment was associated with better recruiting outcomes.

One way to address the first problem is to use a procedure known as instrumental variables. To implement this technique, the researcher needs to identify for each potentially endogenous variable an identifying variable that affects the endogenous variable but is not correlated with the error term of the outcome (recruiting, in this case). Such identifying variables are notoriously difficult to locate—especially when there is more than one potentially endogenous variable—and we did not find any identifying variables for either the number of recruiters or State Guard educational programs.[4]

In discussions with policymakers and in reviewing the literature, we found no consensus as to whether these theoretical possibilities were likely to be a problem (see Cotterman, 1986; Polich, Dertouzos, and Press, 1986; Murray and McDonald, 1999). The degree to which these issues are problems is related to how recruiting resources are in fact allocated and how much variation there is across states and time.

We explored the potential endogeneity of recruiters empirically using two strategies. First, we estimated the NPS model with and without the potentially endogenous policy variables to ascertain the degree to which the coefficient estimates of the other variables changed. This would indicate the degree to which the inclusion of these policy variables altered and hence, possibly biased other coefficient estimates. Second, we estimated a model of the number of recruiters in which we regressed the number of recruiters on the other variables in the model and recruiting outcomes. The results of these exercises are reported in the next chapter along with the complete set of results.

In the next section, we describe our efforts to obtain data for the analysis. In addition, we describe in more detail how we construct our dependent variables and what explanatory variables we chose for each model.

---

[4] Note that because we include state and year fixed effects, omitting policy variables or other variables that do not vary across states or across years is not a violation of the second condition.

Data and Sample Description

Both the NPS and the PS samples have 408 observations, with an observation being based on a state in a given fiscal year. We use all 50 states along with the District of Columbia and fiscal years 1992 to 1999. We do not use data prior to 1992 because we could not obtain several variables in our analysis prior to that year. Similarly, data are not available in a consistent fashion beyond 1999 for many of our variables, including the dependent variables.

We used nearly a dozen different sources to create the data used in this analysis. These include both military data sets, generally maintained by the Defense Manpower Data Center (DMDC), and a number of civilian data sets. The source and creation of each specific variable we use is described in detail in Appendix B.

Weighting Grouped Data and Heteroskedasticity

We must address two additional estimation issues for the models we estimate: the weighting strategy to use and the potential for heteroskedasticity. There are at least three potential conventional approaches we could have taken to weighting the grouped data in our analysis. The first approach is to consider each observation to represent the number of people represented in the outcome. Operationally, we would use the actual number of youths potentially likely to enlist (the denominator of the dependent variable) as the weight. Thus, if a state-FY observation were based on the decisions of 1,000 18-year-olds, then we would assume that we actually have 1,000 people (with independently and identically distributed unexplained propensities to enlist into the military) represented in that one state-FY observation. The second approach is to weight each observation by the percentage that the population for a given state FY represents out of the sum of the population for all state-FY observations in the data. This assigns a fraction as the weight for each observation. The third approach is to ignore the number of people the observation represents, so that each state–fiscal year observation is counted as only one observation. The downside of the first approach is that people in a state may have correlated unexplained propensities to enlist into the military. Thus, using 1,000 as the number of people represented in the state-FY observation would overstate how many independent cases are truly represented in the observation. The downside of the second and third approaches is that there is little difference in the contribution unusually small and large states make to the coefficient estimates, so you do not take into account the greater contribution of larger states to overall recruiting outcomes. Note that the first and second weighting schemes would produce the same estimates of the coefficients, but different estimates of the standard errors.

While none of these approaches is ideal, we believe that the first approach is the best method for our models. Greene (2000) indicates that weighting by the number of individuals in a proportions model like the NPS model will actually correct the standard errors of the estimates, which will be understated because they are divided by a factor proportional to the population. However, he warns that when using this weighting approach for an ordinary least squares regression as in the PS model, the standard errors can be very small when the population is large.

Another estimation issue we must consider is the potential for the error terms in our model to violate a basic condition in econometrics necessary for obtaining efficient standard error estimates: that the variance of the error terms be constant across observations. Our data may violate this condition because the variance of the error terms may vary with the size of the state. This condition of unequal variance of error terms across observations is known as heteroskedasticity. In the PS model, we might expect that the variance of the number of recruits would be higher for larger states. However, for the NPS model, the variance in the proportion of those who are eligible (eligibles) actually entering active duty or the reserves may be higher for the smaller states because smaller populations tend to have larger variances for data expressed as proportions (Greene, 2000).

As Murray and McDonald (1999) do in their recruiting model, we apply a correction for heteroskedasticity for the PS model. Relative to the standard errors from the noncorrected model, the standard errors in the corrected model increased for 78 of the 81 coefficient estimates and increased by 18.5 percent, on average. The maximum increase was 51 percent. However, for the PS model, the standard errors were so small relative to the coefficient estimates that the correction made little difference in significance levels. For the proportions model used in the NPS estimates, the weighting scheme described above, where each states' observation would be weighted by the denominator of the proportion, should correct for the fact that the errors would vary with state size (Greene, 2000).

CHAPTER FIVE

Results

This chapter reports the results of the empirical analysis. All analyses are conducted with the state FY as the unit of observation. The NPS model estimates are weighted by the projected number of 18-year-olds in that state FY,[1] and the PS model estimates are weighted by the number of active duty exits in the previous year.

We estimated NPS models for both high-quality accessions and all accessions. The results of these estimates varied substantially. Given the emphasis of recruiting policy and the previous literature on high-quality accessions, our discussion focuses on the high-quality results. We report the results for all accessions in Appendix C.[2]

Non-Prior-Service Results

In Table 5.1, we provide the descriptive statistics of the variables in the NPS analysis. We report both the standard deviation of the variables and their adjusted standard deviation, which controls for state and year effects.[3] The adjusted standard deviation represents the variation in the variables after the state and year effects are taken out. Given that we control for state and year effects in the model, this more accurately depicts the variation we use to identify the relationship between the variables and recruiting.

The number of NPS reserve accessions in a state in a year averages around one-and-a-half percent of 18-year-olds, while the number of active duty accessions averages nearly 5 percent. There are slightly more than 3 recruiters per 1,000 18-year-olds on average in each state, with the 10th and 90th percentiles being 2.4 and 4.1 recruiters, respectively, per 1,000 teenagers. The other recruiting policy variables we include are State Guard educational benefits. Across the years in our sample, about half the states offered tuition deferments to reservists while slightly less than a third offered other types of educational benefits to reservists, such as loan repayment.

Some variables lose more variation than others when we control for state and year effects, as shown in Table 5.1. The percentage of eligible NPS individuals who enter the reserves loses more than two-thirds of its variation after controlling for state and year. The employer size variables, the wage variables, and the family variables lose the least variation with

---

[1] This projection was described in the previous chapter.

[2] Note that Alabama is excluded from the tables in Appendix C because it is used as the reference group.

[3] That is, we regress each variable on the year and state dummy variables and then calculate the standard deviations of the residuals of those equations. The mean of the residual would be zero for all variables.

Table 5.1
Descriptive Statistics for the NPS Model (Weighted by the Projected Population of 18-Year-Olds in a State FY)

Variable	Mean	Standard Deviation	Adjusted Standard Deviation
Share of NPS eligibles entering the reserves	0.014	0.007	0.002
Share of NPS eligibles entering active duty	0.048	0.011	0.003
Share of NPS high-quality eligibles entering the reserves	0.015	0.008	0.002
Share of NPS high-quality eligibles entering active duty	0.062	0.017	0.005
Recruiters per 1,000 18-year-olds	3.160	0.632	0.213
Recruiters per 1,000 18-year-olds squared	10.387	4.117	1.495
Unemployment rate	5.686	1.549	0.453
Percentage of 25- to 65-year-olds with a bachelor degree	0.266	0.046	0.014
Percentage of 25- to 65-year-olds who are veterans	0.132	0.022	0.008
Percentage of 18-year-olds who are black	0.147	0.101	0.003
Percentage of 18 year olds who are Hispanic	0.133	0.137	0.003
Percentage of workers in government	0.030	0.019	0.006
Percentage of workers in firms with more than 25 people	0.717	0.035	0.015
Average tuition at 4-year public universities (1999 dollars)	2754.6	924.8	166.2
HOPE-like scholarships available	0.043	0.203	0.133
States with reserve tuition benefits program	0.499	0.500	0.237
States with reserve educational incentives	0.302	0.459	0.175
Married with children	0.048	0.029	0.019
Male high school graduate wage, second quartile (median)	12.052	1.467	0.598
Natural log of male high school graduate median wage	2.482	0.123	0.051
Male college graduate wage, second quartile (median)	17.983	2.319	1.128
Natural log of male college graduate median wage	2.881	0.131	0.064

the controls for state and year effects, while the tuition and demographic variables (percentage black and percentage Hispanic) lose the most variation. This implies that while controlling for state and year, there will be little variation in tuition and demographic variables. This indicates it will be less likely that these variables will help explain recruiting outcomes, but it does not necessarily mean they will have no effect.

The Potential Endogeneity of Recruiting Policy Variables

As discussed above, there is some concern about the potential endogeneity of the policy variables, which are the number of active duty recruiters per capita and the State Guard educational incentives. We estimated specifications with and without these policy variables and generally obtained the same substantive results in both cases. While some of the coefficients from the two specifications were statistically different, they were generally of the same sign and general order of magnitude. For example, one of the largest changes observed between the two specifications was for the unemployment rate. The unemployment rate coefficient estimate for active duty enlistment in the specification without recruiters was 0.024 (with a standard error of 0.005) while the estimate was 0.016 (with a standard error of 0.005) in the specification with recruiters. For most of the other variables, we obtain similar coefficient estimates regardless of whether we include the policy variables or not. We present the specification that includes the policy variables below, and we report the specification with no policy variables in Appendix C.

A second way we examined the potential endogeneity of the active duty recruiters variable was to estimate a regression of the number of recruiters per capita (specifically, per 1,000 18-year-olds) on other explanatory variables in the model. The results of this regression would indicate the degree to which the number of recruiters per capita was determined by factors in the model as opposed to factors outside the model. We find that as a group, the other variables in the model do explain the number of recruiters per capita quite well (see Table 5.2). The regression of the number of recruiters per 1,000 18-year-olds on the other variables explains a very large amount of variation in the number of recruiters (R^2 of nearly 0.9). Note, however, that the variables that are explaining the number of recruiters are primarily the state and year dummy variables. Very few of the other variables in the model are statistically significant, and in specifications that did not include the state and year effects, the variation explained by the model dropped by two-thirds (to an R^2 of about 0.3). This corroborates the results in the descriptive statistics table above, which showed that the standard deviation of the recruiter variable dropped substantially when adjusted for state and year. One of the variables that is important in explaining the number of recruiters is the unemployment rate: Holding other variables constant, an increase in the unemployment rate of a percentage point is associated with 0.07 more recruiters per 1,000 18-year-olds.

In general, this regression demonstrates that the number of recruiters in a state in a year is likely to be highly related to the number of recruiters in that state in the past, perhaps with some deviation driven by changes in the unemployment rate. This is consistent with the way recruiting policymakers reported assigning recruiters to locations when we interviewed individuals at recruiting commands as part of the first phase of this project.

Table 5.2
Coefficient Estimates for Model of Recruiters Per Capita

Variable	Coefficient Estimate	Standard Error	Significance
Median high school graduate wage	0.312	0.221	
Median college wage	−0.085	0.178	
Unemployment rate	0.072	0.026	***
Percentage of adults with a bachelor degree	−0.675	0.855	
Percentage of adults who are veterans	0.125	1.389	
Percentage black	9.157	4.334	**
Percentage Hispanic	0.639	3.693	
Average tuition at 4-year public universities	0.026	0.073	
Percentage married with children	−1.926	0.612	***
Percentage of workers in government	−0.375	1.895	
Percentage of workers in firms with more than 25 people	0.853	0.788	
Reserve tuition benefits program	0.042	0.067	
Reserve limited scholarship program	−0.013	0.091	
HOPE-like scholarships available	−0.157	0.091	*
R-squared = 0.90			

NOTES: The dependent variable is the number of recruiters per 1,000 18-year-olds. Year and state dummy variables are also included in this regression. Significance levels: *** 0.01 level, ** 0.05 level, and * 0.10 level.

In sum, we find evidence that other variables in the model can explain the number of recruiters in a state in a year but that once we have controlled for state and year, the other variables explain little of the additional variance. Given that we are estimating a fixed-effects model that identifies effects from deviations within a state across years, we will be using within-state deviations in the number of recruiters to identify the effect of recruiters on enlistment. Furthermore, adding the recruiting policy variables to the enlistment model does not change the substantive findings. However, the fact that the number of recruiters depends on the unemployment rate indicates that results from the enlistment model with or without the number of recruiters may be inconsistent or biased. The similar substantive findings in these two specifications suggest that these findings can be trusted, but the magnitudes must be considered with caution. With similar results across the specifications, we present as our preferred specification, a model of NPS enlistment that includes the recruiting policy variables along with state and year controls.

High-Quality Enlistment Estimates

We present the marginal effects estimates from the grouped multinomial logit model, which includes active duty enlistment, reserve enlistment, and no enlistment as the choice alternatives (see Table 5.3). The marginal effects estimates indicate the change in the fraction making those choices given a one unit change in the variable or, for variables that take on values

Table 5.3
Marginal Effects for NPS Model

Variable	Percentage Point Change in Fraction of Eligibles Enlisting		Percentage Change in Fraction Enlisting	
	Active	Reserves	Active	Reserves
Recruiters per capita	0.016 ***	0.004 ***	25.3%	28.6%
Recruiters per capita squared	−0.001 ***	−0.001 ***	−2.1%	−5.1%
Median high school graduate wage	−0.000 ***	−0.000 ***	−2.1%	−5.1%
Median college graduate wage	0.000 ***	0.000	0.0%	−0.0%
Unemployment rate	0.001 ***	0.001 ***	1.4%	6.5%
Percentage of adults with a bachelor degree	−0.000 ***	−0.001 ***	−0.2%	−1.2%
Percentage of adults who are veterans	−0.000	0.000 **	−0.1%	0.6%
Percentage black	0.001 ***	0.000 ***	1.0%	2.1%
Percentage Hispanic	0.004 ***	0.000 **	6.4%	1.3%
Average tuition at 4-year public universities	0.005 ***	−0.001 ***	7.8%	−6.4%
Percentage married with children	0.000 ***	0.000	0.2%	0.0%
Percentage of workers in government	−0.000	−0.000 *	−0.1%	−0.6%
Percentage of workers in firms with more than 25 people	−0.000 ***	−0.000 ***	−0.5%	1.1%
Reserve tuition benefits program	0.003 ***	0.002 ***	5.0%	11.7%
Reserve limited scholarship program	0.003 ***	−0.001 **	4.6%	−4.0%
HOPE-like scholarships available	−0.002 ***	−0.000 **	−3.3%	−3.3%

NOTES: Coefficient estimates and standard errors for all variables are reported in Appendix C, Table C.1. Significance levels: *** 0.01 level, ** 0.05 level, and * 0.10 level.

of one or zero, the change in the probability when the variable changes from zero to one.[4] Given that the dependent variable is relatively small, we have also included in another column the percentage change in the dependent variable that this marginal effect represents. The asterisks indicate the level of statistical significance of the coefficient estimates, which are reported in Appendix C, Table C.1.

As expected, the number of active duty recruiters has a sizeable and significant effect on the number of active duty accessions in a state. Our hypothesis about the effect of adding recruiters on high-quality reserve accessions in a state was ambiguous, depending on the relative size of the linear and quadratic recruiter terms. We find that the effect of adding an additional recruiter per 1,000 18-year-olds—on average about a 30 percent increase—depends on where in the recruiter density distribution the recruiter is added. If the number of recruiters per 1,000 18-year-olds is two and another recruiter is added to reach three, which is about the average, active duty and reserve recruiting both increase—by 15.5 percent and 3.9 percent, respectively. So at this level of recruiter density, both active duty and reserve recruiting benefit from an additional recruiter, but active duty recruiting benefits much more. However, adding one more recruiter when the recruiter density is three per 1,000 18-year-olds yields different results. At this level of recruiter density, active duty recruiting is still helped, but at a lower rate—active duty enlistments rise 10.6 percent. In contrast, in this case reserve enlistments decline by 5.4 percent. In general, at lower levels of recruiter density, both active duty and reserve recruiting benefit from the addition of another recruiter, but as the number of recruiters rise, this benefit becomes successively smaller and eventually becomes negative for reserve recruiting in the range where we observe the bulk of recruiter density. These findings imply that empirical models that examine the effect of active duty recruiters on active duty recruiting only could overstate the net benefits of increasing the number of active duty recruiters from a total force perspective, because reserve recruiting could decrease. Thus, when comparing the cost-effectiveness of various active duty recruiting resources, the effect on reserve recruiting should be considered as well.

The findings regarding the State Guard educational benefit policies are also somewhat ambiguous. While we would expect greater reserve enlistments in states with more generous benefits, it is not clear whether more generous benefits would lead to more or fewer active duty enlistments. We find that states with tuition deferment programs for State Guard enlistees realize more enlistments in both active duty and the reserves. These results suggest that states with a State Guard college tuition benefit yield about a 5 percent higher fraction enlisting in active duty and 11.7 percent higher fraction enlisting in the reserves. However, for the nontuition benefits, we find a positive effect on active duty recruiting but a negative effect on reserve recruiting, with the latter running counter to theory.

Among the economic and demographic variables, the unemployment rate is one of the most important predictors of a state's recruiting success. A higher unemployment rate is associated with better recruiting outcomes for active duty and the reserves. A one percentage point increase in the unemployment rate is estimated to increase the number of reserve recruits by almost 7 percent and the number of active duty recruits by about one-and-a-half percent.

---

[4] For logged variables, the marginal effects estimates represent the change in the fraction making the choice for a 1 percent change in the variable.

Only a handful of other economic and demographic variables are found to yield sizeable changes in recruiting outcomes. States with more minorities produce more recruits, all else held constant. Since blacks have been overrepresented throughout the All-Volunteer Force era, it is not surprising that states with a higher fraction of black residents have better recruiting outcomes. However, Hispanics have generally been underrepresented in the All-Volunteer Force, so it is somewhat surprising that states with a higher fraction of Hispanic residents have better recruiting outcomes and that the magnitude of the Hispanic marginal effect is as large or larger than that of the black marginal effect in percentage terms.

The estimated marginal effects on active duty recruiting of $1,000 of college tuition and having a HOPE-like scholarship are 3.2 and 7.9 percent, respectively. These are consistent with attending college being a substitute to active duty. The predicted effect of these factors on reserve recruiting is ambiguous because attending college could be a substitute or complement to reserve recruiting. The estimates do not lend insight into this, since an increase in tuition has a negative effect on reserve recruiting while having a HOPE-like scholarship also has a predicted negative effect on reserve recruiting.

Prior-Service Results

The variables included in the PS model are the same as the variables in the NPS model, with a few exceptions. First, we include active duty exits in the current year and the three previous years in the PS model. Second, we include the percentage of those exiting active duty in the state who are black or Hispanic rather than the percentage of youth in the state from those groups. Third, we do not include the variable indicating whether the state has a program like the HOPE scholarship because these programs are directed at current high school graduates. Finally, we do not include the number of active duty recruiters in the model. The means, standard deviations, and adjusted standard deviations for these additional variables are in Table 5.4.

Table 5.4
Descriptive Statistics (Weighted by the Number of Active Duty Exits This Year and Last Year)

Variable	Mean	Standard Deviation	Adjusted Standard Deviation
Number of PS accessions to active duty	2,237	1,552	332
Natural logarithm of the number of PS accessions to active duty	7.434	0.814	0.078
Exits this year	4816.4	3388.4	514.8
Exits last year	4982.3	3438.3	505.9
Exits 2 years ago	5259.6	3585.7	574.6
Exits 3 years ago	5448.9	3659.9	624.45
Percentage of those exiting active duty who are black	0.149	0.105	0.011
Percentage of those exiting active duty who are Hispanic	0.063	0.071	0.010

Table 5.5 presents the results from the ordinary least squares model for PS accessions. All of the coefficient estimates are statistically significant, in part because of the weighting system used, in which the number of cases within a state FY is the number of active duty exits that year and the prior year (see Greene, 2000). It is important to keep in mind that we control for FY and state, so the coefficient estimates in the model are based on variation within states over time.

What stands out as the primary driver of PS accessions is the number of active duty exits over the last few years. With the dependent variable (the number of PS accessions) and the number of active duty exits in natural logarithm form, the coefficient estimates indicate that a 1 percent increase in the number of active duty exits this year and last year is associated with, respectively, a 0.60 and 0.25 percent higher number of PS accessions into the reserve this year. The number of those exiting active duty two and three years ago is also related to PS enlistments, but the size of these effects is smaller, as would be expected.

The economic variables are also important determinants of PS accessions. A one percentage point increase in the unemployment rate is associated with 1.4 percent more accessions. A 1-percent increase in the median wage of high school graduates is associated with a 0.15 percent increase in PS accessions. This may seem counterintuitive, as one would expect that higher wages would lead to fewer enlistments. However, higher wages for high school

Table 5.5
Coefficient Estimates for PS Model

Variable	Coefficient Estimate	Standard Error
Active duty exits this year	0.604	0.002
Active duty exits the previous year	0.252	0.002
Active duty exits 2 years ago	0.070	0.002
Active duty exits 3 years ago	0.128	0.002
Unemployment rate	0.014	0.000
Log median male high school graduate wage	0.146	0.001
Log median male college graduate wage	−0.040	0.001
Percentage of adults with a bachelor degree	−0.082	0.004
Percentage of adults who are veterans	−0.145	0.006
Percentage of active duty exits black	0.249	0.005
Percentage of active duty exits Hispanic	−0.181	0.005
Average tuition at 4-year public universities	0.043	0.000
Percentage married with children	0.184	0.003
Percentage of workers in government	−1.099	0.007
Percentage of workers in firms with 25 or more people	0.317	0.003
States with State Guard tuition program	−0.018	0.000
States with other State Guard educational incentives	−0.014	0.000
R-squared = 0.9947		

NOTE: Coefficients and standard errors for the constant term and the FY and state dummy variables are reported in Appendix Table C.3.

graduates would discourage PS separatees from attending college, which could increase the availability of them for reserve service. The coefficient estimates on the college graduate wage quartiles are tiny.

The variables that characterize the civilian workplace also have large coefficients. Consistent with theory, the greater the average firm size, the more PS enlistments in the state. We expected that having more government workers would be associated with greater PS enlistment, but the coefficient estimate for the fraction of the workforce employed in the government sector is large and negative.

The estimates for a number of the demographic variables also are the opposite of what the theory predicted. For example, one would expect that the number of PS enlistments would be greater in areas with a greater veteran population, but we obtain a negative coefficient for the fraction veteran variable. We also estimate negative coefficients for the variables that indicate the percentage of the population who are black or Hispanic. The estimate for the percentage of the population with a bachelor degree is negative, which is consistent with theory.

Family characteristics also appear to be important for the number of PS accessions. Increases in the percentage of young males from a state who are married with children are associated with a higher number of accessions. Perhaps, those who have children are in greater need of extra income, which the reserves can provide.

The model we estimated for PS enlistment explains almost all the variation in PS recruiting, as demonstrated by the extremely high R-squared of 0.99 for the model. However, the estimates of many of the policy, economic, and demographic variables do not conform to theoretical expectations. It is likely that the large number of state and FY dummy variables and the large effective sample generated by the weighting scheme are responsible for the high degree of variation the model explains. We conclude that the PS model generates too many implausible results to be considered reliable.

There are a couple of possible explanations for the implausible results generated by this model. One possible cause is that the remaining variation in some of the explanatory variables, after controlling for state and FY, is mostly due to sampling error rather than actual population changes. Another possible explanation is that measurement error is affecting the results. In constructing the dependent variable for the PS model and variables that represent active duty exits, we experienced problems with the quality of the data including home state. It may be the case that our attempts to mitigate problems with these data were not able to eliminate sufficient measurement error to produce quality estimates. We believe that efforts to obtain improved data and further explore improving the PS model are fruitful areas for additional research.

CHAPTER SIX

Conclusions

These results demonstrate the feasibility and utility of estimating NPS reserve enlistment supply models akin to those that have been estimated for active duty over the last two decades. However, the results call into question the transferability of these types of models to the PS reserve context. The results from the NPS model were consistent with theory, plausible, and generated a number of new and useful findings. In contrast, many of the results from the PS model were counter to theory.

Weaknesses in the PS model are likely the result of several factors. One is measurement error problems in the data used in the estimation. For example, there are numerous conceptual and practical problems inherent in identifying the relevant home state for PS individuals. Another is that building on the modeling approach used for active duty aggregate recruiting models may not be a reasonable characterization of the PS enlistment decision. We believe that developing a different modeling approach from one based on the dichotomous choice of whether to join the reserves could produce a better fit for PS reserve recruiting. In particular, a joint modeling of the decisions to leave active duty and to enter the reserves may improve the model. Developing an alternative approach to estimating models of PS enlistment would be a valuable area for future research. This study is the only attempt to model PS recruiting of which we are aware.

The NPS enlistment estimates generated a number of new and useful findings. The approach to modeling NPS enlistments we implemented in this monograph is novel in a number of ways. It recognizes that the active force and the reserves compete against each other for recruits. In addition, it includes variables that have not been taken into account in other studies. One type of variable recognizes the importance of some increasing sources of competition for reservists' time: college attendance and family demands. Another type of variable characterizes State Guard educational benefits.

Another contribution of this monograph is an examination of the effects of the potential endogeneity of policy variables on the estimates. We find evidence of the endogeneity of the number of reserve recruiters per capita, but we also find that the results of the model are not altered substantially by including the potentially endogenous variables. An open question is the potential bias due to the fact that we do not have data on some policy variables and therefore may have "omitted variable bias." Collecting data on additional policy variables, such as advertising and mission strategies, and including these variables in reserve models should be a priority for future reserve recruiting research.

We found that the policy variables included in the NPS model have sizeable and significant effects on both active duty and reserve recruiting. While the reserve recruiting policy variables tended to benefit both reserve recruiting and active duty recruiting, the active duty policy variable we included benefited active duty recruiting, but beyond levels of average recruiter density, partially at the expense of reserve enlistments. State Guard educational bene-fits were associated with higher active duty enlistments in that state, with tuition deferment also contributing to higher reserve enlistments. For states with more active duty recruiters per capita, active duty enlistments were higher, but reserve enlistments were lower. This suggests that active duty and reserve forces are competing for the same recruits rather than a situation where active duty and reserve recruiting efforts complement each other.

This finding merits more in-depth cost-effectiveness analysis, because it has impor-tant implications for resourcing decisions. Also, it is possible that current estimates overstate active duty recruiter effectiveness because they do not take into account the potential nega-tive consequences of these recruiters on reserve enlistments. Because of the quadratic effect of active duty recruiters that we find on reserve recruiting—where active duty recruiters initially benefit reserve recruiting, but that after a point additional active duty recruiters harm reserve recruiting—it may be the case that the optimal level of active duty recruiters from a total force perspective is slightly below the optimal number of recruiters from purely an active duty perspective.

Among the economic and demographic variables in the NPS model, we found three types of variables that exhibited a strong relationship to recruiting. Not surprisingly, the un-employment rate—one of the traditional staples of recruiting models—was one of these vari-ables. Increases in the unemployment rate were associated with substantial rises in both ac-tive duty and reserve recruiting.

We also found that a state's minority representation was among the most important predictors of recruiting success. The fraction of Hispanics as well as the fraction of blacks in the population of 18-year-olds was highly predictive of NPS recruiting outcomes, with states having more minorities enlisting more recruits in both active duty and the reserves. Hispan-ics are the fastest growing segment of the youth population, and the fact that they have been underrepresented in recruiting has been a source of concern for recruiting policymakers. These results suggest that recruiting has in fact been somewhat successful in areas where there are more Hispanics. Given the importance of the Hispanic population to future re-cruiting outcomes, it would be valuable to undertake more detailed exploration of recruiting outcomes for areas with strong Hispanic representation.

The cost of college was the third factor that we found to be important. States that of-fered "HOPE-like" scholarships—scholarships to in-state colleges or universities for indi-viduals performing well in that state's high schools—enlisted a smaller fraction of young people in both active duty and the reserves. These scholarships were initiated over the last decade and have been enormously popular in their respective states. These findings add to a growing literature that points to the importance of college as a source of competition for re-cruits and the need to monitor college policies that might affect recruiting.

We also found that in-state tuition levels were related to NPS recruiting, although the results were slightly different from the findings regarding the HOPE-like scholarships. States with higher tuition had a higher fraction of youths enlisting in active duty but a lower fraction enlisting in the reserves. This pattern of results might indicate that college is a substi-tute for active duty but could be a complement to reserve service. That is, one cannot com-bine college and active duty, but one can combine college and reserve service. So college at-tendance and active duty enlistment may respond in opposite directions to tuition increases, but college attendance and reserve service may respond in the same direction. There may be opportunities to develop more explicit strategies to attract reservists who would like to couple college and military service.

Also noteworthy are the economic and demographic variables that did not have a strong relationship to recruiting. We did not find that characteristics of civilian employers had a large impact on NPS recruiting, nor did we find a big relationship between enlistment and "influencer" characteristics, such as the population size of college graduates or veterans. We also found little association between enlistment and the potential demand for men's time from home responsibilities.

Component-Specific Recruiting Outcomes

As with reserve recruiting numbers, overall DoD reserve recruit quality trends mask the quality shortfalls and achievements of the individual components. While the mean percentage of NPS reserve recruits with a high school diploma was 89 percent over the FY 1990–2000 period, the individual components averaged between 77 percent for the Naval Reserves and 98 percent for the Marine Corps Reserves (see Figure A.1). The deviations from the average were not huge over the period: The DoD average had a standard deviation of 3 percent, while the individual services' standard deviations were all under 6 percent.

Similarly, we observe differences across the components in the average percentage who scored in the top half of the AFQT score distribution, or in categories I–IIIA (Figure A.2). In this case, the percentage of NPS reserve recruits scoring in this range averaged 66 percent over the FY 1990–2000 period. However, the individual averages for the compo-

Figure A.1
Average Percentage of NPS Reserve Recruits Who Have High School Diplomas in FY 1990–2000, by Component

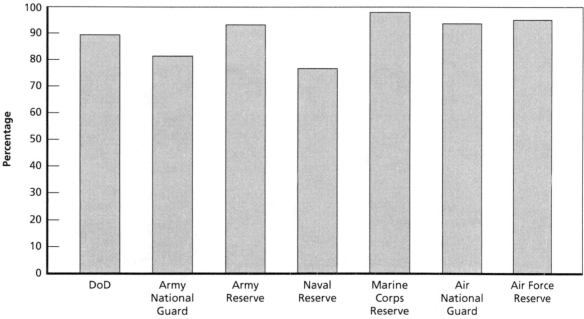

SOURCE: Based on data sent to the authors from Accession Policy, Office of the Under Secretary of Defense for Personnel and Readiness.
RAND MG202-A.1

Figure A.2
Average Percentage of NPS Reserve Recruits Scoring in AFQT Categories I–IIIA in FY 1990–2000, by Component

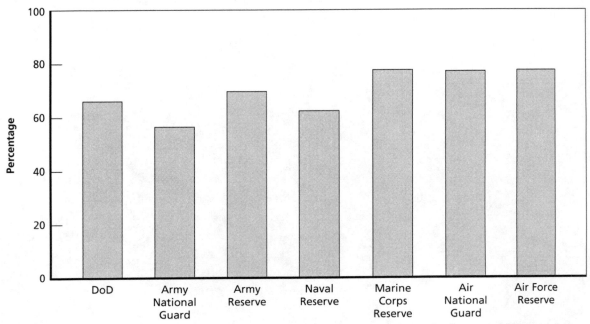

SOURCE: Based on data sent to the authors from Accession Policy, Office of the Under Secretary of Defense for Personnel and Readiness.
RAND *MG202-A.2*

nents ranged from 56 percent for the Army National Guard to 77 percent for the Marine Corps Reserve, Air National Guard, and Air Force Reserve. Again, the fluctuations around these means were relatively modest.

Descriptions of Data Sources

We use data from multiple sources in this analysis. This appendix describes our efforts in collecting the data, how we constructed the dependent and independent variables, and our samples.

Data Requirements

To estimate the model, the recruiting data would ideally be available

- by year or month
- by a consistent geographic unit, such as a state, representing home of origin for the recruit
- for not only recruiting outcomes, but also policy variables, such as advertising expenditures
- using standardized definitions across services, years, and geographic areas
- for a large number of years in the past.

As discussed earlier, a subsidiary consideration for the data was the data's capacity to be used in a predictive model. This consideration added another desirable feature to this list: updated regularly and in a timely fashion, so that future years of data could be added to the model.

Collecting the Data

Given these requirements, we considered two sources of recruiting data for NPS accessions into the reserve: data obtained from each component and administrative data from DMDC files.

Collecting data from each component proved to be the weaker approach for a number of reasons. We were able to acquire the needed data from only four of the six components. Furthermore, the definitions used were not consistent across the components, making pooling data infeasible. For example, the U.S. Naval Reserve listed the state from which the person was recruited as the home state of the recruit. Thus, states with large Naval presences, such as Alaska, had a higher share of recruits listing Alaska as their home state than would be reasonable. However, for the analysis we needed to record the variable as the home state rather than the duty state, because, for the most part, the recruit considers the economic opportunities and other factors based on his home state and not where he is heading for duty or where he is currently on duty. Either of these data shortcomings—the difficulty of obtaining the data from all components or the inconsistent data definitions across the components—would make this source of data untenable.

Instead, we used recruiting data from several DMDC data sets. The primary files were the Reserve Components Common Personnel Data System (RCCPDS) and the corresponding Transaction File, which are administrative data sets maintained by DMDC. The RCCPDS file is an inventory of the members of each component of the reserve at a given point in time, along with demographic characteristics and information pertaining to their military careers. The Transaction File indicates who enters into and exits from the reserve components.

These files are put together based on personnel file reports from each of the six components. Rather than having the state from which a person was recruited, the files have the home state of record. In addition, the files have personal identification numbers, which we used to match to other DMDC data sets to identify the person's original home state and to determine whether the person was a high-quality recruit.

For our purposes, the data for the reserve recruiting policy instruments were even more problematic than the recruiting data from the components. Only one of the six components was able to provide data on the number of recruiters by state, but the data went back to only 1996. For advertising expenditures by state, again only one component had such data, but back to only 1999. Thus, we were unable to include as part of our analysis estimates of the effect of the number of reserve recruiters or advertising expenditures on the number of accessions.

NPS Reserve Accessions Data

For NPS reserve recruits the first home state we used was from the Military Entrance Processing Station (MEPS) file. The MEPS file includes information on recruits when they first sign up to enlist in the military. If the home state was not available on the MEPS file, then we used the home state from the RCCPDS file, taking the first one that we observe (in case the home state changes over time). After matching the files, the home state was still missing for 10.0 percent of the reserve accessions between 1992 and 1999 that we observed.[1]

NPS Active Duty Accessions Data

We obtained the number of active duty accessions by state and fiscal year from several sources. We started by examining monthly extracts of DMDC's PERSTEMPO database to

---

[1] We explored whether we could use the duty state as the home state for NPS reserves to use when the home state was missing. We found this to be infeasible for two main reasons. First, 63 percent of those with a missing home state were in the U.S. Marine Corps Reserve (with missing component being the next highest category for 20 percent), and almost all of them had Missouri as their home state. This was probably because Missouri is a central clearinghouse for Marine Corps recruits. Second, from a match of NPS accessions into components other than the U.S. Marine Corps Reserve with a valid state from MEPS and a valid duty state, 24 percent had different states listed as their home of record and their duty state. Thus, the error rate was too high for us to use this information.

determine all the people who entered active duty.[2] We excluded anyone who had been on any previous PERSTEMPO data set, which would have indicated that they were actually PS accessions to active duty. Because PERSTEMPO data do not have the home-of-record state, we matched the accessions to three other DMDC data sets that contain the home state. First, we used data from MEPS. The state from this data set would override the state information from the other data sets, except for those who did not have a home state recorded in the MEPS file. Second, we examined annual extracts from the Active Duty Master File (ADMF), which is the source from which PERSTEMPO data are created. ADMF has information for everyone in active duty as of a specific date—we used September data. With this data set, however, we still may have been missing some who accessed into the military one fiscal year but left before September. Third, we also matched the accessions from PERSTEMPO data to DMDC's "Loss" files, which contain information for every person who leaves active duty.

After merging these files, the home state was still missing for only 1.4 percent of active duty accessions, after excluding people born in other countries or in U.S. territories.

Identifying High-Quality NPS Recruits

To determine whether a person entering active duty was a high-quality accession, we combined information from the MEPS and PERSTEMPO files. The person must have had at least a high school diploma and an AFQT percentile score of 50 or more. Our high-quality numbers match fairly well with the overall numbers that DoD publishes, as shown in Table B.1. For the last year, 1999, it appears that we undercounted the actual number of high-quality accessions, probably because the missing data had not yet been updated.

For NPS reserve accessions, we had even more difficulty in identifying which accessions were high quality. While there is an indicator for whether the person was in AFQT category I to IIIA (i.e., having an AFQT percentile score of at least 50), there was no indicator for whether a person completed high school. However, we used the AFQT criterion only, which requires the assumption that all people with an AFQT score of 50 or more completed high school. Certainly, we expected that we would label some who were not officially high quality as being high quality. Despite this expectation, it turned out that we underestimated the percentage of high-quality recruits in each year for NPS reserve accessions, as shown in Table B.1. Our numbers are fairly consistent relative to the official numbers until 1997, when there is a sharp decrease in our counts of NPS high-quality accessions. The number appears to slightly recover in 1998 and recover even more in 1999. The reason for this drop off is due to missing data, with most of the drop off coming from enormous increases from 1996 to 1997 in the percentage of people who were not Tier 1 for only the U.S. Army Reserve and the Army National Guard.

While an option for dealing with these missing data was to eliminate one or two years from our analysis, we believed that they should be included. We concluded that the nonmissing data for those "bad" years probably still had some useful information. Furthermore, the systematic pattern in the bad data appeared to be across components.

---

[2] The reason we did not use MEPS to start was that MEPS data include people who did not complete the accession process.

Table B.1
**Percentage of NPS Accessions to Active Duty and the
Reserves Who Are High Quality: Comparison of Official
Statistics and Statistics from Our Sample**

Year	Active Duty		Reserve	
	Our Sample	Official Number	Our Sample	Official Number
1992	0.74	0.73	0.56	0.67
1993	0.68	0.66	0.64	0.69
1994	0.68	0.66	0.61	0.65
1995	0.67	0.66	0.62	0.67
1996	0.66	0.64	0.61	0.68
1997	0.64	0.63	0.44	0.66
1998	0.62	0.61	0.50	0.64
1999	0.53	0.57	0.57	0.68

PS Reserve Accessions Data

To identify who entered the reserves as a PS recruit and which state they came from, we again used several files from DMDC. We started with the transaction file to identify who entered the reserves with prior military duty. These included those who had prior service in the active forces as well as the reserve forces, but we cannot perfectly distinguish between which type of PS duty a person had.

With those PS accessions, we matched them to the following DMDC files, listed in order of priority for capturing the home state:

1. MEPS
2. ADMF
3. Active Duty Loss Files
4. RCCPDS for current tour of duty (for those without an active duty record)
5. RCCPDS for previous tour of duty (for those without an active duty record).

If there was no home state listed in the MEPS file, the ADMF, and the Loss Files and if there was no record of the person in our active duty files, we assumed that the person's PS duty was in the reserves. In those cases, we used the home-of-record state indicated on the RCCPDS files. We looked not only at the state from the current reserve tour of duty, but also at the state from the past tours of duty if we had the data for them. For those who were active duty and had no home state on the active duty sources of data, we did not use the home state from the RCCPDS data. The reason for this was that the home state we observed for the reserves was different in many instances from the home state from which recruits came.[3] In fact, the home-of-record state in the RCCPDS data was the last active duty state in many cases. We believe that the original home state was the state that would be more rele-

---

[3] Of the (420,195) prior-service accessions who had a valid home state from MEPS data and a home-of-record state from the RCCPDS, 32.4 percent had them listed as different states.

vant for economic opportunities and other factors than the last active duty state. We may have assigned some people to the wrong state from which they consider civilian alternatives. For example, those who permanently settle after active duty in their duty state or some state other than their original home state may indeed consider the economic opportunities and other factors in their new state. However, by assigning people to their original home state, we avoid the problem of there being too many people coming from states with active duty bases. For example, Alaska has a disproportionately high number of PS accessions into the reserves (especially the U.S. Naval Reserve) because many people stationed in Alaska for active duty were coded as having Alaska as their home state. Yet, most of these individuals would probably consider the economic conditions and other factors from their true home state rather than those from Alaska when determining whether to enter the reserves.

Using the reserves' listed home state for those who do not show up in the active duty files reduced the number with a missing home state from 15.3 percent to 2.3 percent.

Dependent Variables

For the NPS model, as mentioned earlier, we have two dependent variables: the ratio of the number of accessions into the reserves to the predicted number of 18-year-olds and the ratio of the number of accessions into active duty to the predicted number of 18-year-olds. To predict the number of people at age 18 in a given state, we use U.S. Census Bureau numbers for the number of 17-year-olds in the state from the year before.[4] The reason for using the number of 17-year-olds as a proxy for the number of 18-year-olds the following year instead of just using the number of 18-year-olds that year was that we were trying to capture the alternative choices to joining the military, such as attending college and entering the civilian labor force. And, once people turn 18, they are more likely to move to another state for work, college, or the military. Thus, using the actual number of 18-year-olds as the basis would be drawing people based on the choice they made rather than the opportunities available to them. For this reason, we did not include the number of people aged 19, 20, etc. in a state, even though people accessing into the military are often older than 18. We rely on the assumption that the pool of potential NPS recruits into active duty and the reserves moves over time with the predicted number of 18-year-olds in the state. We further justify this strategy with the fact that the most common age for accessions is 18.

For high-quality accessions, we divide the predicted number of 18-year-olds by two as an approximation of the number of 18-year-olds who would be high quality. Given that most youths who score in the upper half of the AFQT distribution are likely to have graduated from high school, we believe this is a reasonable estimate. As discussed in Cotterman (1986), the important aspect of this assumption is that the fraction of youth who are high quality remains constant over the period, which seems plausible. Scaling the numerator is important for appropriately scaling the coefficient estimates and standard errors.

The dependent variable for the NPS model is the natural logarithm of the number of people with a given original home state who enter the reserves in a given year.

---

[4] These were obtained from the U.S. Census Bureau web site (http://www.census.gov/population/estimates/state/sasrh/).

Independent Variables

We describe the creation of each of the explanatory variables here and summarize variable descriptions and sources in Table B.2.

Economic Factors

We calculated the annual state unemployment rates (based on fiscal years) from the monthly unemployment rates from the Bureau of Labor Statistics web site. This serves as our primary economic variable. We created the other economic variables from various years of the March CPS. The other variables include the medians of the wage distribution for men: (1) for high school graduates with no college and (2) for four-year college graduates who had no post-graduate schooling.

The male median wages are based on people aged 25 to 54 who had positive hours worked in the given calendar year. The wage data were calculated as the earnings from the previous calendar year divided by the total hours worked (the product of the average hours per week and the weeks worked). Because the March CPS reports the earnings, hours, and weeks worked from the prior calendar year, we used the following year's information on wages and hours for a given year's observation. The high school median wages are based on those who have a high school diploma and no college at all. Likewise, the college wage medians are based on those who have completed four years of college and no more.

The CPS does not include active duty military personnel in the files, so the results should not be affected by military characteristics in states with a large military presence.

Demographic Factors

We calculated the percentage of the eligibles (predicted 18-year-olds) who are black and the percentage who are Hispanic from U.S. Census Bureau data. As with predicting the number of 18-year-olds for the NPS dependent variable, we used the projected number of black and Hispanic 18-year-olds for a given year based on the number of 17-year-olds from the previous year.

Influencer Variables

The role-model factors are calculated from the CPS. We considered all 25- to 65-year-olds and determined what percentage of them were veterans and what percentage completed at least four years of college. We considered using just parents of teenagers from the CPS to measure these percentages, but the sample was too small, causing larger fluctuations in these variables than what we would reasonably expect. Using 25- to 65-year-olds without any restrictions on being a parent increased the sample enough to provide much more reasonable percentages and steady trends over time.

Civilian Workforce Characteristics

For the percentage of the population who work in the government, we used the percentage of employed 25- to 54-year-olds who work in the governmental sector, calculated from the CPS. We used this same sample to compute the firm-size variables. The CPS breaks down firm size into six categories: 1–9, 10–25, 26–99, 100–499, 500–999, and 1,000 or more employees. We divide these into three categories: 1–25, 26–99, and 100 or more employees.

Table B.2
Variable Descriptions and Sources

Variable	Description	Source(s)
Percentage of NPS eligibles entering reserves	Number of NPS accessions into the reserves divided by the projected number of 18-year-olds from that state	U.S. Census Bureau, RCCPDS, Reserve Transaction file
Percentage of NPS eligibles entering active duty	Number of NPS accessions into active duty divided by the projected number of 18-year-olds from that state	U.S. Census Bureau, PERSTEMPO, ADMF
Number of PS accessions to reserves	Number of people entering the reserves who had prior active duty or reserve duty	RCCPDS, Reserve Transaction file
Number of active duty recruiters per capita	Number of recruiters per 1,000 18-year-olds	DMDC
Number of active duty exits from previous years	Number of people who exited active duty in the current, the previous, and the prior 2 FYs	PERSTEMPO
Unemployment rate	Percentage of the labor force who are unemployed	Bureau of Labor Statistics web site
Percentage of workers with a bachelor degree	Percentage of 25- to 65-year-olds who have completed 4 years of college	CPS
Percentage of workers who are veterans	Percentage of 25- to 65-year-olds who are veterans	CPS
Percentage black	Percentage of projected 18-year-olds from a state who are black	U.S. Census Bureau
Percentage Hispanic	Percentage of projected 18-year-olds from a state who are Hispanic	U.S. Census Bureau
Percentage of active duty separatees who are black	Percentage of black people who separate from active duty in the given FY	PERSTEMPO, RCCPDS, Reserve Transaction file
Percentage of active duty separatees who are Hispanic	Percentage of Hispanic people who separate from active duty in the given FY	PERSTEMPO, RCCPDS, Reserve Transaction file
Percentage of workers in government	Percentage of employed 25- to 54-year-olds who work in the governmental sector	CPS
Percentage of workers in firms with at least 25 people	Percentage of 25- to 54-year-olds who indicate that the size of their firm is 25 people or more	CPS
Average tuition at 4-year public universities	Average tuition at 4-year public universities in the state	U.S. Department of Education, various years
Full educational benefits	Indicator for whether the State Guard offers full tuition coverage	Smith and Gordon, 1992–1999
Partial educational benefits	Indicator for whether the State Guard offers partial tuition coverage	Smith and Gordon, 1992–1999
Limited educational benefits	Indicator for whether the State Guard offers loan forgiveness or limited scholarships without tuition assistance	Smith and Gordon, 1992–1999
HOPE-like scholarship available	Indicator for whether the state had a merit-based scholarship program with general eligibility criteria, a large number of students served, and at least public tuition costs paid for	Education Commission of the States (www.ecs.org)
Married with children	Percentage of 18- to 24-year-old males who are heads of households, who are married, and who have children	CPS
Male high school graduate median wage	Median wage for male 25- to 54-year-old employed workers with a high school diploma and no more schooling	CPS
Male college graduate median wage	Median wage for male 25- to 54-year-old employed workers with a college degree and no more schooling	CPS

Educational Opportunities

The tuition numbers come from the *Digest of Education Statistics* from the National Center for Education Statistics (U.S. Department of Education, various years). For the indicator for the merit-based (HOPE-like) scholarships, we created a dummy variable, for which a state-FY observation had a value of one if it had a scholarship that year that had very general eligibility criteria, it served a large number of students in the state, and it paid for at least tuition. This resulted in only four states with eligible programs, and 13 values of one for state-FY pairs in our data—Florida, 1998–1999; Georgia, 1994–1999; Mississippi, 1996–1999; and South Carolina, 1999.

The Current Population Survey

We used the CPS to construct many of our state variables. The CPS is a monthly survey conducted by the Bureau of Labor Statistics, a division within the U.S. Census Bureau. The survey consists of 50,000 households, meant to represent a random sample of the civilian noninstitutional population of the United States. Government officials use the CPS as the source of many official statistics, such as the unemployment rate.

To calculate our statewide variables, we use the March supplement of the CPS, also called the Annual Demographic Survey. The March CPS provides more detailed information on income and work experience.

Coefficient Estimates from the Grouped Multinomial Logit Model

Table C.1
NPS Active Duty Recruits: Results from the Grouped Multinomial Logit Model

Variable	All			High Quality		
	Coefficient Estimate	Standard Error		Coefficient Estimate	Standard Error	
Constant	−3.787	0.184		−3.239	0.165	***
Recruiters per capita	0.300	0.027	***	0.275	0.024	***
Recruiters per capita squared	−2.223	0.380	***	−2.327	0.338	***
Median high school graduate wage	−0.018	0.024		−0.062	0.022	***
Median college graduate wage	0.043	0.019	**	0.053	0.017	***
Unemployment rate	0.009	0.003	***	0.016	0.003	***
Percentage of adults with a bachelor degree	−0.132	0.094		−0.266	0.084	***
Percentage of adults who are veterans	−0.280	0.153	*	−0.084	0.135	
Percentage black	1.780	0.467	***	1.146	0.421	***
Percentage Hispanic	7.159	0.396	***	6.832	0.351	***
Average tuition at 4-year public universities	0.067	0.008	***	0.082	0.007	***
Married with children	0.215	0.068	***	0.220	0.060	***
Percentage of workers in government	0.011	0.207		−0.163	0.184	
Percentage of workers in firms with at least 25 people	−0.613	0.087	***	−0.477	0.078	***
Reserve tuition benefits program	0.061	0.008	***	0.055	0.007	***
Reserve limited scholarship program	0.046	0.010	***	0.048	0.009	***
HOPE-like scholarship available	−0.003	0.009		−0.035	0.009	***
Year 93	−0.001	0.006		−0.106	0.005	***
Year 94	−0.167	0.009	***	−0.279	0.008	***
Year 95	−0.280	0.010	***	−0.390	0.009	***
Year 96	−0.288	0.012	***	−0.416	0.011	***
Year 97	−0.306	0.014	***	−0.475	0.012	***
Year 98	−0.394	0.016	***	−0.573	0.014	***
Year 99	−0.453	0.018	***	−0.811	0.016	***
Alaska	0.072	0.135		0.049	0.122	
Arizona	−1.561	0.164	***	−1.515	0.148	***
Arkansas	0.151	0.054	***	0.080	0.049	*
California	−2.524	0.178	***	−2.555	0.160	***
Colorado	−0.950	0.141	***	−0.893	0.128	***

Table C.1—continued

Variable	All			High Quality		
	Coefficient Estimate	Standard Error		Coefficient Estimate	Standard Error	
Connecticut	−0.801	0.106	***	−0.845	0.096	***
Delaware	−0.341	0.052	***	−0.313	0.047	***
Florida	−0.883	0.081	***	−0.760	0.073	***
Georgia	−0.135	0.019	***	−0.098	0.017	***
Hawaii	−0.445	0.141	***	−0.636	0.127	***
Idaho	−0.022	0.151		−0.007	0.137	
Illinois	−0.867	0.078	***	−0.872	0.070	***
Indiana	−0.056	0.106		−0.071	0.095	
Iowa	0.228	0.142		0.252	0.128	**
Kansas	−0.042	0.122		−0.045	0.110	
Kentucky	0.265	0.113	**	0.174	0.101	*
Louisiana	−0.317	0.028	***	−0.288	0.025	***
Maine	0.519	0.153	***	0.515	0.138	***
Maryland	−0.339	0.031	***	−0.250	0.028	***
Massachusetts	−0.556	0.123	***	−0.628	0.111	***
Michigan	−0.191	0.076	**	−0.217	0.069	***
Minnesota	−0.017	0.138		−0.031	0.124	
Mississippi	−0.276	0.060	***	−0.328	0.054	***
Missouri	0.134	0.090		0.118	0.081	
Montana	0.594	0.153	***	0.671	0.138	***
Nebraska	0.085	0.130		0.107	0.118	
Nevada	−0.788	0.127	***	−0.752	0.114	***
New Hampshire	0.309	0.149	**	0.347	0.134	***
New Jersey	−1.132	0.090	***	−1.167	0.081	***
New Mexico	−2.696	0.216	***	−2.667	0.193	***
New York	−1.202	0.090	***	−1.180	0.081	***
North Carolina	0.009	0.027		0.018	0.024	
North Dakota	0.344	0.151	**	0.419	0.136	***
Ohio	−0.028	0.092		−0.029	0.083	
Oklahoma	0.216	0.109	**	0.190	0.099	*
Oregon	−0.139	0.143		−0.096	0.129	
Pennsylvania	−0.171	0.100	*	−0.187	0.090	**
Rhode Island	−0.414	0.129	***	−0.493	0.116	***
South Carolina	−0.103	0.028	***	−0.073	0.026	***
South Dakota	0.521	0.150	***	0.538	0.135	***
Tennessee	0.024	0.059		0.006	0.053	
Texas	−2.102	0.157	***	−1.999	0.141	***
Utah	−0.357	0.149	**	−0.499	0.135	***
Vermont	0.165	0.152		0.146	0.136	
Virginia	−0.093	0.047	**	−0.045	0.043	
Washington	−0.174	0.135		−0.138	0.122	

Table C.1—continued

Variable	All			High Quality		
	Coefficient Estimate	Standard Error		Coefficient Estimate	Standard Error	
Washington, D.C.	−1.363	0.214	***	−1.245	0.193	***
West Virginia	0.531	0.139	***	0.386	0.125	***
Wisconsin	−0.122	0.119		−0.096	0.107	
Wyoming	0.106	0.151		0.181	0.136	

NOTE: Significance levels: *** 0.01 level, ** 0.05 level, and * 0.10 level.

Table C.2
NPS Reserve Recruits: Results from the Grouped Multinomial Logit Model

Variable	All			High Quality		
	Coefficient Estimate	Standard Error		Coefficient Estimate	Standard Error	
Constant	−4.890	0.325	***	−5.278	0.311	***
Recruiters per capita	0.313	0.042	***	0.307	0.038	***
Recruiters per capita squared	−4.844	0.600	***	−5.319	0.555	***
Median high school graduate wage	0.004	0.042		−0.132	0.040	***
Median college graduate wage	−0.078	0.034	**	−0.024	0.033	
Unemployment rate	0.086	0.005	***	0.067	0.005	***
Percentage of adults with a bachelor degree	−0.462	0.169	***	−1.185	0.159	***
Percentage of adults who are veterans	0.476	0.258	*	0.622	0.242	**
Percentage black	−0.390	0.838		2.235	0.813	***
Percentage Hispanic	0.231	0.759		1.716	0.724	**
Average tuition at 4-year public universities	−0.050	0.015	***	−0.060	0.014	***
Married with children	0.260	0.115	**	−0.020	0.109	
Percentage of workers in government	−1.189	0.357	***	−0.598	0.339	*
Percentage of workers in firms with at least 25 people	1.091	0.148	***	1.085	0.140	***
Reserve tuition benefits program	0.081	0.014	***	0.122	0.013	***
Reserve limited scholarship program	−0.053	0.018	***	−0.037	0.017	**
HOPE-like scholarship available	−0.015	0.018		−0.036	0.018	**
Year 93	−0.193	0.010	***	−0.084	0.009	***
Year 94	−0.250	0.015	***	−0.214	0.014	***
Year 95	−0.296	0.017	***	−0.245	0.016	***
Year 96	−0.265	0.020	***	−0.214	0.019	***
Year 97	−0.317	0.023	***	−0.611	0.022	***
Year 98	−0.252	0.026	***	−0.386	0.025	***
Year 99	−0.037	0.029		−0.058	0.028	**
Alaska	−0.184	0.241		0.566	0.234	**
Arizona	−1.218	0.305	***	−0.679	0.294	**

Table C.2—continued

Variable	All			High Quality		
	Coefficient Estimate	Standard Error		Coefficient Estimate	Standard Error	
Arkansas	0.425	0.096	***	0.684	0.093	***
California	−1.407	0.337	***	−1.092	0.323	***
Colorado	−1.051	0.261	***	−0.208	0.252	
Connecticut	−0.089	0.195		0.618	0.189	***
Delaware	0.105	0.092		0.489	0.089	***
Florida	−0.900	0.152	***	−0.595	0.146	***
Georgia	−0.520	0.034	***	−0.414	0.033	***
Hawaii	0.415	0.253		1.179	0.246	***
Idaho	−0.201	0.273		0.789	0.265	***
Illinois	−0.552	0.145	***	−0.051	0.140	
Indiana	−0.267	0.192		0.398	0.186	**
Iowa	0.351	0.256		1.349	0.248	***
Kansas	0.009	0.222		0.836	0.215	***
Kentucky	−0.576	0.202	***	0.128	0.196	
Louisiana	−0.174	0.050	***	−0.151	0.048	***
Maine	−0.009	0.275		1.161	0.267	***
Maryland	0.008	0.055		0.196	0.052	***
Massachusetts	−0.005	0.224		0.837	0.218	***
Michigan	−1.101	0.139	***	−0.486	0.135	***
Minnesota	0.103	0.249		1.180	0.242	***
Mississippi	0.234	0.106	**	−0.268	0.103	***
Missouri	−0.296	0.164	*	0.384	0.159	**
Montana	0.295	0.274		1.519	0.266	***
Nebraska	0.032	0.235		0.903	0.228	***
Nevada	−0.991	0.233	***	−0.413	0.224	*
New Hampshire	−0.294	0.271		0.827	0.263	***
New Jersey	−0.598	0.167	***	−0.188	0.162	
New Mexico	−0.569	0.408		−0.342	0.392	
New York	−0.765	0.170	***	−0.389	0.164	**
North Carolina	−0.408	0.049	***	−0.287	0.047	***
North Dakota	0.675	0.270	**	1.872	0.261	***
Ohio	−0.747	0.167	***	0.029	0.162	
Oklahoma	0.156	0.196		0.904	0.191	***
Oregon	−0.354	0.259		0.549	0.251	**
Pennsylvania	−0.365	0.182	**	0.434	0.177	**
Rhode Island	0.044	0.232		0.790	0.226	***
South Carolina	−0.053	0.050		−0.088	0.048	*
South Dakota	0.563	0.269	**	1.712	0.261	***
Tennessee	−0.534	0.105	***	−0.228	0.102	**

Table C.2—continued

Variable	All			High Quality		
	Coefficient Estimate	Standard Error		Coefficient Estimate	Standard Error	
Texas	−1.070	0.299	***	−0.893	0.287	***
Utah	−0.154	0.268		0.933	0.260	***
Vermont	0.447	0.275		1.604	0.267	***
Virginia	−0.137	0.087		0.231	0.085	***
Washington	−0.645	0.245	***	0.234	0.238	
Washington, D.C.	0.270	0.381		−0.942	0.369	**
West Virginia	−0.306	0.246		0.653	0.238	***
Wisconsin	−0.176	0.215		0.730	0.209	***
Wyoming	−0.075	0.270		0.964	0.262	***

NOTE: Significance levels: *** 0.01 level, ** 0.05 level, and * 0.10 level.

Table C.3
Comparison of Policy Versus Nonpolicy Variables for High-Quality NPS Model for Active Duty Recruits

Variable	With Policy Variables			Without Policy Variables		
	Coefficient Estimate	Standard Error		Coefficient Estimate	Standard Error	
Constant	−3.239	0.165	***	−3.068	0.157	***
Recruiters per capita	0.275	0.024	***	—	—	
Recruiters per capita squared	−2.327	0.338	***	—	—	
Median high school graduate wage	−0.062	0.022	***	−0.024	0.021	
Median college graduate wage	0.053	0.017	***	0.043	0.017	**
Unemployment rate	0.016	0.003	***	0.025	0.003	***
Percentage of adults with a bachelor degree	−0.266	0.084	***	−0.317	0.084	***
Percentage of adults who are veterans	−0.084	0.135		−0.097	0.135	
Percentage black	1.146	0.421	***	2.242	0.416	***
Percentage Hispanic	6.832	0.351	***	6.916	0.351	***
Average tuition at 4-year public universities	0.082	0.007	***	0.085	0.007	***
Married with children	0.220	0.060	***	0.017	0.059	
Percentage of workers in government	−0.163	0.184		−0.053	0.184	
Percentage of workers in firms with at least 25 people	−0.477	0.078	***	−0.437	0.077	***
Reserve tuition benefits program	0.055	0.007	***	0.062	0.007	***
Reserve limited scholarship program	0.048	0.009	***	0.051	0.009	***
HOPE-like scholarship available	−0.035	0.009	***	−0.052	0.009	***
Year 93	−0.106	0.005	***	−0.124	0.005	***
Year 94	−0.279	0.008	***	−0.317	0.007	***
Year 95	−0.390	0.009	***	−0.399	0.009	***
Year 96	−0.416	0.011	***	−0.409	0.011	***

Table C.3—continued

Variable	With Policy Variables			Without Policy Variables		
	Coefficient Estimate	Standard Error		Coefficient Estimate	Standard Error	
Year 97	−0.475	0.012	***	−0.480	0.012	***
Year 98	−0.573	0.014	***	−0.538	0.014	***
Year 99	−0.811	0.016	***	−0.764	0.015	***
Alaska	0.049	0.122		0.307	0.121	**
Arizona	−1.515	0.148	***	−1.204	0.146	***
Arkansas	0.080	0.049	*	0.181	0.048	***
California	−2.555	0.160	***	−2.413	0.159	***
Colorado	−0.893	0.128	***	−0.556	0.126	***
Connecticut	−0.845	0.096	***	−0.745	0.095	***
Delaware	−0.313	0.047	***	−0.214	0.046	***
Florida	−0.760	0.073	***	−0.559	0.072	***
Georgia	−0.098	0.017	***	−0.120	0.017	***
Hawaii	−0.636	0.127	***	−0.448	0.126	***
Idaho	−0.007	0.137		0.277	0.135	**
Illinois	−0.872	0.070	***	−0.824	0.070	***
Indiana	−0.071	0.095		0.127	0.095	
Iowa	0.252	0.128	**	0.459	0.127	***
Kansas	−0.045	0.110		0.116	0.110	
Kentucky	0.174	0.101	*	0.344	0.101	***
Louisiana	−0.288	0.025	***	−0.359	0.025	***
Maine	0.515	0.138	***	0.979	0.135	***
Maryland	−0.250	0.028	***	−0.237	0.028	***
Massachusetts	−0.628	0.111	***	−0.490	0.110	***
Michigan	−0.217	0.069	***	−0.094	0.068	
Minnesota	−0.031	0.124		0.104	0.123	
Mississippi	−0.328	0.054	***	−0.593	0.053	***
Missouri	0.118	0.081		0.311	0.081	***
Montana	0.671	0.138	***	1.099	0.136	***
Nebraska	0.107	0.118		0.343	0.117	***
Nevada	−0.752	0.114	***	−0.472	0.113	***
New Hampshire	0.347	0.134	***	0.743	0.133	***
New Jersey	−1.167	0.081	***	−1.181	0.080	***
New Mexico	−2.667	0.193	***	−2.397	0.193	***
New York	−1.180	0.081	***	−1.146	0.081	***
North Carolina	0.018	0.024		0.083	0.024	***
North Dakota	0.419	0.136	***	0.567	0.134	***
Ohio	−0.029	0.083		0.197	0.082	**
Oklahoma	0.190	0.099	*	0.471	0.097	***
Oregon	−0.096	0.129		0.280	0.127	**

Table C.3—continued

Variable	With Policy Variables			Without Policy Variables		
	Coefficient Estimate	Standard Error		Coefficient Estimate	Standard Error	
Pennsylvania	−0.187	0.090	**	0.026	0.089	
Rhode Island	−0.493	0.116	***	−0.281	0.115	**
South Carolina	−0.073	0.026	***	−0.071	0.026	***
South Dakota	0.538	0.135	***	0.778	0.133	***
Tennessee	0.006	0.053		0.088	0.053	*
Texas	−1.999	0.141	***	−1.805	0.140	***
Utah	−0.499	0.135	***	−0.425	0.133	***
Vermont	0.146	0.136		0.435	0.135	***
Virginia	−0.045	0.043		0.088	0.042	**
Washington	−0.138	0.122		0.181	0.121	
Washington, D.C.	−1.245	0.193	***	−1.835	0.191	***
West Virginia	0.386	0.125	***	0.725	0.123	***
Wisconsin	−0.096	0.107		0.038	0.107	
Wyoming	0.181	0.136		0.609	0.134	***

NOTE: Significance levels: *** 0.01 level, ** 0.05 level, and * 0.10 level.

Table C.4
Comparison of Policy Versus Nonpolicy Variables for High-Quality NPS Model for Reserve Recruits

Variable	With Policy Variables			Without Policy Variables		
	Coefficient Estimate	Standard Error		Coefficient Estimate	Standard Error	
Constant	−5.278	0.311	***	−4.672	0.304	***
Recruiters per capita	0.307	0.038	***	—	—	
Recruiters per capita squared	−5.319	0.555	***	—	—	
Median high school graduate wage	−0.132	0.040	***	−0.157	0.039	***
Median college graduate wage	−0.024	0.033		−0.007	0.032	
Unemployment rate	0.067	0.005	***	0.068	0.004	***
Percentage of adults with a bachelor degree	−1.185	0.159	***	−1.210	0.159	***
Percentage of adults who are veterans	0.622	0.242	**	0.612	0.242	**
Percentage black	2.235	0.813	***	1.920	0.810	**
Percentage Hispanic	1.716	0.724	**	2.135	0.721	***
Average tuition at 4-year public universities	−0.060	0.014	***	−0.051	0.014	***
Married with children	−0.020	0.109		0.121	0.108	
Percentage of workers in government	−0.598	0.339	*	−0.428	0.338	
Percentage of workers in firms with at least 25 people	1.085	0.140	***	0.922	0.139	***
Reserve tuition benefits program	0.122	0.013	***	0.128	0.013	***
Reserve limited scholarship program	−0.037	0.017	**	−0.026	0.017	

Table C.4—continued

Variable	With Policy Variables			Without Policy Variables		
	Coefficient Estimate	Standard Error		Coefficient Estimate	Standard Error	
HOPE-like scholarship available	−0.036	0.018	**	−0.028	0.018	
Year 93	−0.084	0.009	***	−0.087	0.009	***
Year 94	−0.214	0.014	***	−0.221	0.013	***
Year 95	−0.245	0.016	***	−0.251	0.016	***
Year 96	−0.214	0.019	***	−0.226	0.019	***
Year 97	−0.611	0.022	***	−0.618	0.022	***
Year 98	−0.386	0.025	***	−0.402	0.025	***
Year 99	−0.058	0.028	**	−0.082	0.027	***
Alaska	0.566	0.234	**	0.470	0.234	**
Arizona	−0.679	0.294	**	−0.881	0.293	***
Arkansas	0.684	0.093	***	0.653	0.092	***
California	−1.092	0.323	***	−1.304	0.322	***
Colorado	−0.208	0.252		−0.380	0.251	
Connecticut	0.618	0.189	***	0.533	0.189	***
Delaware	0.489	0.089	***	0.457	0.089	***
Florida	−0.595	0.146	***	−0.773	0.145	***
Georgia	−0.414	0.033	***	−0.404	0.033	***
Hawaii	1.179	0.246	***	1.045	0.245	***
Idaho	0.789	0.265	***	0.673	0.264	**
Illinois	−0.051	0.140		−0.112	0.140	
Indiana	0.398	0.186	**	0.345	0.185	*
Iowa	1.349	0.248	***	1.249	0.247	***
Kansas	0.836	0.215	***	0.753	0.214	***
Kentucky	0.128	0.196		0.087	0.195	
Louisiana	−0.151	0.048	***	−0.129	0.048	***
Maine	1.161	0.267	***	0.839	0.264	***
Maryland	0.196	0.052	***	0.172	0.052	***
Massachusetts	0.837	0.218	***	0.746	0.217	***
Michigan	−0.486	0.135	***	−0.511	0.135	***
Minnesota	1.180	0.242	***	1.080	0.241	***
Mississippi	−0.268	0.103	***	−0.218	0.102	**
Missouri	0.384	0.159	**	0.339	0.158	**
Montana	1.519	0.266	***	1.329	0.264	***
Nebraska	0.903	0.228	***	0.816	0.228	***
Nevada	−0.413	0.224	*	−0.561	0.223	**
New Hampshire	0.827	0.263	***	0.687	0.262	***
New Jersey	−0.188	0.162		−0.286	0.161	*
New Mexico	−0.342	0.392		−0.619	0.391	
New York	−0.389	0.164	**	−0.470	0.163	***

Table C.4—continued

Variable	With Policy Variables			Without Policy Variables		
	Coefficient Estimate	Standard Error		Coefficient Estimate	Standard Error	
North Carolina	−0.287	0.047	***	−0.284	0.047	***
North Dakota	1.872	0.261	***	1.728	0.260	***
Ohio	0.029	0.162		−0.034	0.161	
Oklahoma	0.904	0.191	***	0.800	0.190	***
Oregon	0.549	0.251	**	0.372	0.250	
Pennsylvania	0.434	0.177	**	0.361	0.176	**
Rhode Island	0.790	0.226	***	0.694	0.225	***
South Carolina	−0.088	0.048	*	−0.119	0.048	**
South Dakota	1.712	0.261	***	1.590	0.260	***
Tennessee	−0.228	0.102	**	−0.239	0.102	**
Texas	−0.893	0.287	***	−1.082	0.286	***
Utah	0.933	0.260	***	0.750	0.259	***
Vermont	1.604	0.267	***	1.494	0.266	***
Virginia	0.231	0.085	***	0.158	0.084	*
Washington	0.234	0.238		0.117	0.237	
Washington, D.C.	−0.942	0.369	**	−0.837	0.367	**
West Virginia	0.653	0.238	***	0.523	0.237	**
Wisconsin	0.730	0.209	***	0.667	0.208	***
Wyoming	0.964	0.262	***	0.736	0.260	
Log likelihood	−4534489			−4534807		

NOTE: Significance levels: *** 0.01 level, ** 0.05 level, and * 0.10 level.

Table C.5
Coefficient Estimates for PS Model: Year and State Variables

Variable	Coefficient Estimate	Standard Error
Intercept	−1.567	0.011
Year 93	−0.116	0.001
Year 94	−0.112	0.001
Year 95	−0.196	0.001
Year 96	−0.196	0.001
Year 97	−0.174	0.001
Year 98	−0.203	0.001
Year 99	0.065	0.001
Alaska	0.152	0.004
Arizona	−0.218	0.002
Arkansas	0.099	0.001
California	−0.209	0.002

Table C.5—continued

Variable	Coefficient Estimate	Standard Error
Colorado	–0.237	0.002
Connecticut	–0.076	0.002
Delaware	0.097	0.003
Florida	–0.331	0.001
Georgia	–0.210	0.001
Hawaii	0.187	0.003
Idaho	0.013	0.002
Illinois	–0.280	0.001
Indiana	–0.167	0.001
Iowa	–0.029	0.002
Kansas	0.363	0.002
Kentucky	–0.132	0.001
Louisiana	–0.250	0.001
Maine	–0.081	0.002
Maryland	0.059	0.001
Massachusetts	0.202	0.002
Michigan	–0.418	0.002
Minnesota	0.001	0.002
Mississippi	0.000	0.001
Missouri	–0.068	0.001
Montana	–0.032	0.002
Nebraska	–0.034	0.002
Nevada	–0.329	0.003
New Hampshire	–0.095	0.002
New Jersey	–0.066	0.001
New Mexico	–0.004	0.003
New York	–0.128	0.002
North Carolina	–0.239	0.001
North Dakota	–0.040	0.004
Ohio	–0.339	0.002
Oklahoma	0.084	0.001
Oregon	–0.297	0.002
Pennsylvania	–0.197	0.002
Rhode Island	0.180	0.003
South Carolina	–0.227	0.001
South Dakota	–0.109	0.003
Tennessee	–0.125	0.001
Texas	–0.256	0.002
Utah	0.575	0.003
Vermont	–0.052	0.004
Virginia	–0.244	0.001
Washington	–0.192	0.002
Washington, D.C.	0.688	0.004

Table C.5—continued

Variable	Coefficient Estimate	Standard Error
West Virginia	0.043	0.002
Wisconsin	−0.042	0.002
Wyoming	−0.142	0.003

References

Asch, Beth J., *Reserve Supply in the Post-Desert Storm Recruiting Environment,* Santa Monica, Calif.: RAND Corporation, MR-224-FMP, 1993.

Asch, Beth J., M. Rebecca Kilburn, and Jacob A. Klerman, *Attracting College-Bound Youth into the Military: Toward the Development of New Recruiting Policy Options,* Santa Monica, Calif.: RAND Corporation, MR-984-OSD, 1999.

Bianchi, Suzanne M., "Maternal Employment and Time with Children: Dramatic Change or Surprising Continuity?" *Demography,* Vol. 37, No. 4, November 2000, pp. 401–414.

Cotterman, Robert F., *Forecasting Enlistment Supply: A Time Series of Cross Sections Model,* Santa Monica, Calif.: RAND Corporation, N-3252-FMP, 1986.

Dertouzos, James N., *Recruiter Incentives and Enlistment Supply,* Santa Monica, Calif.: RAND Corporation, R-3065-MIL, 1985.

Efron, Bradley, "Regression and ANOVA with Zero-One Data: Measures of Residual Variation," *Journal of the American Statistical Association,* Vol. 73, No. 361, March 1978, pp. 113–121.

Ellis, R. P., G. C. Pope, L. I. Iezzoni, et al., "Diagnosis-Based Risk Adjustment for Medicare Capitation Payments," *Health Care Financing Review,* Vol. 17, No. 3, Spring 1996, pp. 101–128.

Fricker, Ronald D., Jr., *The Effects of Perstempo on Officer Retention in the U.S. Military,* Santa Monica, Calif.: RAND Corporation, MR-1556-OSD, 2002.

Greene, William H., *Econometric Analysis,* New York: Prentice-Hall, Inc., 2000.

Grissmer, David W., Sheila Nataraj Kirby, and Man-Bing Sze, *Factors Affecting Reenlistment of Reservists: Spouse and Employer Attitudes and Perceived Unit Environment,* Santa Monica, Calif.: RAND Corporation, R-4011-RA, 1992.

Hosek, James R., and Christine E. Peterson, *Enlistment Decisions of Young Men,* Santa Monica, Calif.: RAND Corporation, R-3238-MIL, 1985.

Hosek, James R., Christine E. Peterson, and Rick Eden, *Educational Expectations and Enlistment Decisions,* Santa Monica, Calif.: RAND Corporation, R-3350-FMP, 1986.

Hosek, James R., and Mark Totten, *Serving Away from Home: How Deployments Influence Reenlistment,* Santa Monica, Calif.: RAND Corporation, MR-1594-OSD, 2002.

Juster, F. Thomas, and Frank P. Stafford, "The Allocation of Time: Empirical Findings, Behavioral Models, and Problems of Measurement," *Journal of Economic Literature,* Vol. 29, No. 2, June 1991, pp. 471–522.

Kilburn, M. Rebecca, *Minority Representation in the U.S. Military,* dissertation, Chicago, Ill.: University of Chicago, Department of Economics, 1994.

Kilburn, M. Rebecca, Sheila Nataraj Kirby, C. Christine Fair, and Scott Naftel, unpublished RAND research on trends affecting reserve recruiting.

Kilburn, M. Rebecca, and Jacob A. Klerman, *Enlistment Decisions in the 1990s: Evidence from Individual-Level Data,* Santa Monica, Calif.: RAND Corporation, MR-944-OSD/A, 1999.

Kim, Choongsoo, Gilbert Nestel, Robert L. Phillips, and Michael E. Borus, "The All-Volunteer Force: An Analysis of Youth Participation, Attrition, and Reenlistment," *National Longitudinal Survey of Youth Labor Market Experience Military Studies,* Columbus, Ohio: The Ohio State University, Center for Human Resource Research, May 1980.

Kirby, Sheila Nataraj, and Scott Naftel, *The Effect of Mobilization on Retention of Enlisted Reservists After Operation Desert Shield/Storm,* Santa Monica, Calif.: RAND Corporation, MR-943-OSD, 1998.

Kostiuk, P., and J. Grogan, *Enlistment Supply into the Naval Reserve,* Alexandria, Va.: Center for Naval Analyses, CRM 87-239, 1987.

Manski, Charles F., and David A. Wise, *College Choice in America,* Cambridge, Mass.: Harvard University Press, 1983.

Marquis, M. Susan, and Sheila Nataraj Kirby, *Reserve Accessions Among Individuals with Prior Military Service: Supply and Skill Match,* Santa Monica, Calif.: RAND Corporation, R-3892-RA, 1989.

McFadden, David, "Conditional Logit Analysis of Qualitative Choice Behavior," in P. Zarembka, ed., *Frontiers in Econometrics,* New York: Academic Press, 1973.

———, "Econometric Analysis of Qualitative Response Models," in Zvi Griliches and M. Intrilligator, eds., *Handbook of Econometrics,* Vol. 2, Amsterdam: North-Holland Publishing, 1983.

Mishel, Lawrence, Jaren Bernstein, and Jon Schmitt, *The State of Working America, 1998–1999,* Washington, D.C.: Economic Policy Institute, 1999.

Murray, Michael P., and Laurie L. McDonald, *Recent Recruiting Trends and Their Implications for Models of Enlistment Supply,* Santa Monica, Calif.: RAND Corporation, MR-847-OSD/A, 1999.

Polich, J. Michael, James N. Dertouzos, and S. James Press, *The Enlistment Bonus Experiment,* Santa Monica, Calif.: RAND Corporation, R-3353-FMP, 1986.

Reville, Robert T., *Two Essays on Intergenerational Earnings and Wage Mobility,* dissertation, Providence, R.I.: Brown University, May 1996.

Schmidt, Christoph M., and Klaus F. Zimmermann, "Work Characteristics, Firm Size and Wages," *Review of Economics and Statistics,* Vol. 73, No. 4, November 1991, pp. 705–710.

Shishko, Robert, and Bernard Rostker, "The Economics of Multiple Job Holding," *American Economic Review,* Vol. 66, No. 3, June 1976, pp. 298–308.

Smith, Gary L., and Debra M. Gordon, eds., *National Guard Almanac,* Falls Church, Va.: Uniformed Services Almanac, Inc., various years.

South, Scott J., and Glenna Spitz, "Housework in Marital and Nonmarital Households," *American Sociological Review,* Vol. 59, No. 3, June 1994, pp. 327–347.

Tan, Hong, *Non-Prior Service Reserve Enlistments: Supply Estimates and Forecasts,* Santa Monica, Calif.: RAND Corporation, R-3786-FMP/RA, 1991.

Theil, H., *Economic Forecasts and Policy,* Second Edition, Amsterdam: North-Holland Publishing, 1961.

U.S. Census Bureau, *Statistical Abstract of the United States,* Washington, D.C.: U.S. Government Printing Office, various years.

U.S. Department of Defense, Office of the Assistant Secretary of Defense (Force Management Policy), *Population Representation in the Military Services,* Washington, D.C., various years (a).

U.S. Department of Defense, Office of the Secretary of Defense, Defense Manpower Data Center, *Active Duty Master Files*, Washington, D.C., various years (b).

U.S. Department of Education, National Center for Education Statistics, *Digest of Education Statistics*, various years. Online at http://nces.ed.gov/programs/digest/ (as of July 7, 2005).

Warner, John T., and Beth J. Asch, "The Economics of Military Manpower," in Keith Hartley and Todd Sandler, eds., *Handbook of Defense Economics*, Vol. 1, New York: Elsevier Press, 1995, pp. 349–398.

Warner, John T., Curtis J. Simon, and Deborah M. Payne, *Enlistment Supply in the 1990s: A Study of the Navy College Fund and Other Incentive Programs*, Arlington, Va.: Defense Manpower Data Center, Report No. 2000-015, 2001.

Willis, Robert J., and Sherwin Rosen, "Education and Self-Selection," *Journal of Political Economy*, Vol. 87, No. 5, Part 2, pp. S7–36, October 1979.